AN APOSTOLIC STRATEGY

HOPLON

ACCESSING YOUR WEAPONS TO DELIVER SPIRITUAL WARFARE FROM HEAVENLY PLACES

ZAC BRECKENRIDGE

Dedication

While praying for God's heart for the year 2019, he very clearly laid on my heart legacy. I dedicate this book to my daughter Isabelle. May this establish a legacy which your ministry shall one day thrive. This book was also written with the desire for every future LifeBridger to know why their pastor chose to plant another church in the "City of Churches." May LifeBridge always continue with the legacy with which it was initiated.

Table of Contents

Introduction

For the weapons of our warfare are not of the flesh but have divine power to destroy strongholds. - 2 Corinthians 10:4

Hoplon, the Greek ὅπλον, can accurately be translated as weapon, tool, or instrument. In modern times, the church must become ever more aware that our battles cannot be wasted over physical diversions. Every movement sweeping our nation that is contrary to our Christian core values is not just a trend; it is a spiritual ploy to eradicate Christianity.

The church has been cloaked with both heavenly authority and power as well as gifted with leadership to develop and implement those skills when necessary to stop the aggression of the enemy. However, we cannot enter into battle empty handed. May this book become a hoplon to spiritual warfare in modern times. May it become a training tool, an instrument to help us better understand our significance, and finally a hidden weapon in our arsenal by which we will expand the kingdom of God.

Chapter 1:
Strategic Strategy

To this day, I still remember my favorite toy gun growing up. It was a grey revolver with the ever familiar orange tip on the end of the barrel. No matter the occasion, from cowboys with my cousin to hunting alone by myself out of my bedroom window, it was my go to toy gun. Throughout the years of growing up as a boy in a small town in the South, the prized possession survived much wear and tear. Despite the broken hammer on the back, it still was my favorite.

As I continued to mature, toy guns began to be upgraded: water guns, pop cap guns, and eventually paintball guns. Paintball became a routine event throughout my later teen years. That same cousin became my backup and a couple more friends became my go to comrades to skirt the battle lines alongside. Strategically deployed we all knew our assignment to get the opponents out while covering one another from the oncoming attacks. On more than one occasion during tournament play, I was accused of having my paintball gun set to fully automatic; we were well trained, though not unstoppable.

Honestly, I tended to struggle in

environments where I wasn't a natural leader of some sorts while growing up. Being the oldest of my cousins, I naturally took on this role. However, a lack of much athleticism matched with this flaw kept me from excelling in sports. It always seemed to be unspoken, but in my mind I knew that it was I who led and became the common denominator among friends.

There was a distinction to my adolescent leadership though. I always saw it fit to lead from the middle. While athleticism was not my strongest attribute, I naturally excelled in academia. I remember very early on in class sitting there knowing the answer yet waiting to see if another child could contribute to the discussion. I waited until I had determined in my mind that no one else knew the answer before contributing to the conversation. It was my way of allowing everyone an equal opportunity to participate and to only slightly realign their answers when necessary.

While this may sound to some like the early stages of narcissism, I believe it to be true that not all leaders are trained; some are simply born. I could not deny this gifting or calling upon my life. What these stories do not illuminate was the struggle that I had to own this identity and to understand how this would come to pass within the Kingdom of God. Even though I had strong leadership thoughts, many times they remained just that: thoughts. I was characterised by most of my peers as the "quiet, introverted bookworm" who likely wouldn't do much leading outside of the realm of scholars. I share these thoughts, stories to encourage all that God has created us with a divine purpose and plan along with placing his desires within our hearts.

Psalm 37:4 - Delight yourself in the LORD, and he will give you the desires of your heart.

We must learn to nurture these inner knowings as we mature both physically and spiritually or we will not see our lives fulfill their God-ordained purpose and even worse we will be a lead contributing factor in the church not fulfilling the role it was created to become.

Lesson behind the Strategy

Pastoring a church plant in what many call the post-Christian America has come with many challenges in which neither business school nor seminary could prepare me. Eliminating the struggles of working with people as a factor, there has been one element to the pastoral role that I had no clue would take so much time and attention: warfare.

November 5th, 2017 is a day in church history that will forever shift my ministry. It was on this day that a small church in Sutherland Springs, Texas would have the deadliest service of its existence. That day, an armed man brutally murdered twenty-seven of God's children. That day, I had to trade my grey revolver with the orange snub nose in one more time for an upgrade. I could never have been prepared enough as a shepherd of a church for security and the real threat it opposes to sheep who are under my direct care.

In biblical times, shepherds weren't always considered the most glamorous occupation. Although great leaders such as David had their start as a shepherd, for the most part, this job was considered among the dishonourables. Shepherds were considered by most religious and political leaders as thieves and weren't even allowed to share their testimony in court. Shepherds were also limited in their ability to worship God due to their career. Their job made them unclean, which caused them to have to ritually cleanse themselves before they could enter into the temple for worship. The primary reason shepherds became unclean had little to do with shepherding as we may think of it now. Yes, a shepherd is responsible for insuring the flock has enough vital nutrients and water nearby and being a master statician responsible for noticing if even one member of the herd wandered off. However, the shepherd became unclean when he had to kill.

John 10:11 - I am the good shepherd. The good shepherd lays down his life for the sheep.

Jesus compares his role of tending to the church to the work of a shepherd. As Jesus made this statement, he wasn't merely prophesying his future on the cross; he revealed a crucial attribute of a shepherd's job description. Shepherds, when necessary, would protect the sheep from bears, wolves, or even thieves. Upon entering this battle, the shepherd must come to the sober conclusion that life would be taken: his, the attackers, or the sheep. A good shepherd must be willing to fight to death if that is what it takes to protect the sheep.

Pastoral positions aren't merely tending and feeding the sheep; a good shepherd must be willing to fight to the death to protect the sheep he watches.

As this revelation began to unfold in my life, I took my newly discovered responsibility serious. I grieved over the lives lost in Sutherland Springs, but I also grieved knowing a good shepherd laid down his life that day and the enemy still took some sheep. I also couldn't help but to realize the attack came when the senior shepherd was absent. Consequently, I began to enroll myself in various trainings to equip me to be a better shepherd; to be prepared to lay down my life if necessary to protect my sheep, or to be able to stop an aggressor with the intent of harming God's people.

Learning the Strategy

Over the next three months following this shooting, I enrolled in three different courses to equip me as a protector. The first class that I attended was a basic concealed carry licensing course. The instructor of the course actually waived the fee for pastors, elders, and deacons due to the shooting at Sutherland Springs. I learned the basics of firearm safety and carrying as well as when to know how to respond to deadly force, especially in church settings. He tailored the stories of course to be applicable to church settings. What stood out most to me that day was the fact that a firearm is a tool and the amount of time to respond to an aggressor is limited so I must be alert.

1 Peter 5:8 - Be sober-minded; Be watchful. Your adversary the devil prowls around like a roaring lion, seeking someone to devour.

The next course I enrolled in was an active shooter scenario class that was staged inside of one of the local churches in my area. The security director of the church I pastor attended this course alongside me. We learned how to properly disarm an aggressor as well as crowd management. This course contained a lot of hands-on exercises which gave us the training necessary to be adept and adaptable as a security team. However, our church plant still faced a very serious challenge.

At the time of taking these courses, the church I pastor was still in its early stages of being a church plant. We were settling into our original location, but this location was on a college campus. The campus offered a landmark location in the town we minister in as well as ease in setup time and cost. Yet it was illegal for our security team to be properly armed to stop an aggressor with deadly force even if that situation were to ever become necessary. As in most situations, the campus offered armed security officers which was something we simply could not afford at that time in our church's history. Safety was too far away had a dire need arose; that is until Arkansas changed its laws.

Early into the next year, Arkansas passed a new endorsement to the concealed carry license. This "enhanced" carry license was more practical, lawful, and extensive training which truly prepared an individual to carry a firearm for protection. It is here that I must interject there truly is a difference in defense and protection. The basic course taught me I needed to be able to defend me personally; the enhanced course trained me how to be able to protect those around me that I loved, most importantly the innocent sheep in the house of God.

The collective trainings that I received radically changed my everyday life, but I could not fathom just how drastically they would change my ministry. I began to unwrap the truest meaning of being a shepherd: not the glamorized version I had pictured in seminary. I began to shepherd our people. I began to put the children in the safest classrooms were there to be any disaster. I informed our security team that their role was to be that of a sheepdog - look and smell like sheep but be a dog in the fight. We strategically positioned them throughout the crowds in our services. Perhaps most importantly, I realized that as a believer we all need someone that we can depend on as consistently within the church as I depend on my firearm. My everyday carry goes with me nearly everywhere (unless I'm carrying a backup), every day. I trust the lives of my church members, my family, and even myself with it knowing that even in the darkest of situations it will be by my side ready. That revelation unlocked a new realm of discipleship within our leadership team and eventually our church body.

Living the Strategy

These events, of course, did not merely impact our physicality. I didn't just become more prepared to protect flesh and soul, nor did I just equip our church physically. I also began to unfold the role of shepherds, and other ministerial callings, spiritually. Several Scriptures came to mind in regards to how our Christianity is not merely a one-time prayer of repentance and membership to a Sunday gathering. Truly being Christ-like calls us to encounter both the angelic and demonic; it beckons us to be engaged in the supernatural realm and to commission the angelic in warfare against the demonic.

John 10:10 - The thief comes only to steal and kill and destroy. I came that they may have life and have it abundantly.

James 4:7 - Submit yourselves therefore to God. Resist the devil, and he will flee from you.

Ephesians 6:12 - For we do not wrestle against flesh and blood, but against the rulers, against the authorities, against the cosmic powers over this present darkness, against the spiritual forces of evil in the heavenly places.

These passages reminded me that demonic forces are alive and their impact is real *against* this world. There is not a single time that the demonic realm comes into the life of an individual to benefit them eternally. As we begin to follow Christ, even the devil himself knows and becomes involved in a level of warfare against our lives. He will use unbelievers and sons of disobedience to antagonize followers of Jesus and attempt to make us fall. However, if we do not recognize that our warfare must be brought in the spirit realm, then our efforts to expand the kingdom of God are only a facade that will be destroyed by the works of the enemy.

Upon processing this truth, I began to compile personal teachings and resources into one location: to establish a legacy that could be passed down from one generation to the next in regards to successful battle plans, testimonies, and insight into the strategies the enemy will use against believers supernaturally. This resource is to be a guide from the eyes of a general, a commanding officer, in a war that is not against flesh and blood.

Leading the Strategy

Generals rarely engage in warfare on the frontlines of battle. They provide much more impact by positioning themselves in a place where they can observe the attacks of the enemy and comprise a battle plan to retaliate strategically. Many come to the notion of promotion in Christianity with the mindset of "greater levels, greater devils." While this is reality, it also must be understood that while generals have a greater viewpoint of attacks, they also have more foot-soldiers to protect them and give them space to see and respond to the attacks.

Growing up in the South, I can easily recall two prominent Generals from the Civil War: Ulysses S. Grant and Robert E. Lee. Other than the original Commander in Chief George Washington, these men stood out as the most iconic generals in history. The Civil War was unlike any other skirmish fought by the United States. As the nation was divided, this war perhaps has had the longest intrinsic impact throughout generations. Ulysses S. Grant held the title as reigning champion and

Robert E. Lee, a "hardcore match" fighter from the South, was determined to make a name for himself and quite literally put the South on the map -- or at least that's how my young mind imagined it. Looking back, I wonder now what makes these two men so renown. Denoted as the "bloodiest battle" in American history, it is estimated that over six hundred thousand soldiers died during the Civil War. Reports also allude to the fact that these valiant soldiers who gave their lives for this nation were led by approximately one thousand generals between the Union and Confederate armies combined. Once again, even history books focus their recollection primarily on Ulysses S. Grant and Robert E. Lee. One must ask why these two stood out so highly amongst their peers. Neither Ulysses S. Grant nor Robert E. Lee could have been compared to Goliath in their military conquests. It is not as though either of these two men stood out in battle and slaughtered countless soldiers at their own hands. Likewise, neither Ulysses S. Grant nor Robert E. Lee were akin to David either. They weren't the unnamed little brother who gained fame by taking out the strongest opponent the world had known. No; these men gained their repute because of their military strategy. Had either of these men been on the frontlines of the battle serving as a private, history may have turned out drastically different. The reason our nation is who we are today is largely in part to the strategies these men brought to the table as commanding officers and strategists.

Similar to the lists of Generals from the Civil War, America has long been known for their Generals of the faith as well. William J. Seymour,

Aimee Semple McPherson, Smith Wigglesworth, Kathryn Kuhlman, Oral Roberts, Lester Sumrall, Charles and Frances Hunter, George Jeffreys, F. F. Bosworth, George Whitefield, Charles Finney, William and Catherine Booth, and even the recently late Billy Graham all make the list of Generals of the faith. Those mentioned by no means capture all the generals, but simply are a representation that as many valiant soldiers take on rankings of authority in leading our nation in natural wars so too many valiant Christians take on a role in leading the Church into spiritual warfare. Each individual has a special characterization that makes their ministry and impact unique, yet they were all known for their strategic insights into life as a Christian and how that impacts both God's Kingdom and the Kingdom of Darkness. Any one of them could have lived out their Christianity from the pews, but they would not have made an everlasting impact had they died without learning and operating in spiritual authority. America and the world as we see it has been shaped throughout history by warfare: natural and supernatural. The question each new generation must face is: to what extent will we be involved?

Generals command armies: such a powerful revelation, right? Yet few of us get involved in spiritual warfare on a level much greater than ourselves. We will perform a kamikaze attack on the enemy's camp and then wonder at why we are beaten up by the attacks, especially when we have Job's infamous hedge of protection. At best, we will surround ourselves with a small unit of fellow soldiers for Christ and attempt to infiltrate enemy lines. Generals command armies; generals of the faith, I assert, command both physical and spiritual armies in this warfare that is not against flesh and blood.

Throughout Scripture we see it is a regular occurrence to encounter angelic beings. From Hagar at the well to Jesus sending his angel to provide testimony to the church in Revelation, angels appear repeatedly throughout biblical times. Jesus' ministry is especially tied to the angelic. Mary is promised by an angel that God will overshadow her. The multitude of heavenly hosts show up to the shepherds to inform them of the birth of the Messiah. When the devil stops tempting Jesus after his fast, ministering angels show up.

Matthew 13:41 - The Son of Man will send his angels, and they will gather out of his kingdom all causes of sin and all law-breakers,

Jesus was a commander of the angel armies and so too are we as 'little Christs.' Angelic appearances were even so common in the early church that in Acts 12 as many were gathered together praying for Peter's release from prison they thought it was more likely that his angel would be at the door knocking than that he would actually have been freed. What faith! Yet this reveals to us starkly just how regular and ordinary angelic encounters would have been in the church.

Loosening the Strategy

Once I began to see the regularity of the angelic in the Bible, I had to question myself as to why I had become so desensitized to their presence. Next, I began to realize the pertinence angels have to me fulfilling my ministry. If Jesus needed angels to minister to him, how much more so must I as an imitation of Jesus lean on these supernatural hosts to assist me in expanding his kingdom on earth as they live it in heaven.

Paul provides us much insight as to how the angelic world affects our lives and kingdom work within the book of Ephesians. This book has become my favorite writing in the New Testament and I believe few believers truly uncover its significance. The church at Ephesus was pastored by Timothy who Paul ordained on Pentecost Sunday on his way to Corinth through Macedonia. Timothy, and the church at Ephesus, became a hub for the early church. Timothy's leadership was sought after in the early church as Paul's greatest disciple. Acts, Romans, 1 & 2 Corinthians, Ephesians, Philippians, Colossians, 1 & 2 Thessalonians, Hebrews, and Revelation all mention either Timothy or Ephesus. Paul mentions in his letters to Timothy both Galatians and Titus. John, another apostle who worked in Ephesus, wrote John, 1 John, 2 John, and 3 John, as well as Revelation. James and Jude then become the only non-gospels not influenced by Pastor Timothy of Ephesus. Timothy likely had been trained by Paul in the apostolic and knew how to fulfill offices he wasn't called to (do the work of an evangelist - regardless of the perspective of whether Timothy was a shepherd or an evangelist, he still held one position he did not feel called towards). This should give us great confidence in the letter of Ephesians as being a forerunner teaching on effective prayer within the church.

<u>Loving the Strategy</u>

The church at Ephesus wasn't just a hub for the early church. The Ephesians had a very rich understanding of spiritual warfare. Artemis was the commanding demonic force in that region at the time Paul visited.

Acts 19:28 - When they heard this they were enraged and were crying out, " Great is Artemis of the Ephesians!"

This spirit, as with any, began to rear its head when Paul brings the gospel to Ephesus. This spirit cast confusion on the citizens of Ephesus as Paul's preaching began to make an impact; it stirred up a revolt through Demetrius the silversmith by questioning his income. We see here the demonic alliance with Mammon. Artemis, this Grecian goddess, influenced hunting and was one of the Olympians. If the Apostle Paul and Timothy wanted God's kingdom to be expanded in Ephesus, the first act they had to take was dealing with this regional spirit. Timothy also battled against fear and was exhorted by Paul that deceitful spirits and teachings of demons will cause some to depart from the faith. Pastoral leadership, for Timothy, meant active spiritual warfare. Timothy understood the cruciality of not just proclaiming the gospel and putting together programs, but truly pastoring the people of Ephesus both physically and spiritually.

Aside from Paul's two personal letters to Timothy, he writes one letter directed to the entire local church. Paul reminds the believers they have been gifted with salvation which rescued them from following the prince of the power of the air, a spirit which Paul says still influences disobedient sons. He then begins to unveil in this letter the strategy of church leadership beginning with Christ. He reminds the believer that they are one with Christ being built into one body, essentially that there is one Church which meets in many various locations. Paul asserts that the entire structure of the house of God is being built on the foundation of the apostles and prophets whose ministry treats Christ as a cornerstone for expansion direction. The heavenly strategy, Paul informs, was revealed to the apostles and prophets by the Spirit and he encourages the church that he prays for their understanding of God. As Paul begins to reiterate over and over that the body is to be united as one, he then interjects that we are also divinely divided. Paul informs that Christ gifted the church with five offices of leadership by which the saints are being equipped individually and the body is being built up. Paul gives some insight into practical Christianity and what it looks like to walk in love. He concludes his letter with the infamous armor of God.

In the paragraph discussing the armor of God, Paul informs the believer of the importance of being spiritually prepared for warfare. He reveals to the church that it is the scheme of the devil to empower a demonic hierarchy which is the antithesis of the five leadership positions Christ gave. We can see, and will look at more in depth in later chapters, how these two sets of spiritual influencers both compare and align in their purpose of expanding their respective kingdoms here on earth. Recall in Ephesians 4, the purpose of Christ gifting this leadership model to the church:

to equip the saints for the work of ministry, for building up the body of Christ, until we all attain to the unity of the faith and of the knowledge of the Son of God, to mature manhood, to the measure of the stature of the fullness of Christ, so that we may no longer be children, tossed to and fro by the waves and carried about by every wind of doctrine, by human cunning, by craftiness in deceitful schemes. Rather, speaking the truth in love, we are to grow up in every way into him who is the head, into Christ, from whom the whole body, joined and held together by every joint with which it is equipped, when each part is working properly, makes the body grow so that it builds itself up in love. - Ephesians 4:12-16

       May this resource be used to edify the five offices that Christ gifted the church and equip the saints for the work of ministry. May we all trade in our prized toy revolver one more time to receive the weapons of our warfare.

Chapter 2:
Five Fold Ministers

Growing up in the South, it seemed as though every guy I knew and even a few of the girls hunted to some extent. At the age of eight, several life changing events occurred: my dad's cousin and best friend passed away in a car accident, I was baptized, and I went deer hunting with my dad for the first time.

My dad would always come home with whatever sort of game he had harvested and show my mother and I as I grew up. When I turned eight, he asked if I would like to join him for a deer hunt. I went with him and as he tells the story we weren't there even thirty minutes before a small buck came along and he had the opportunity to harvest it. I was a very excited little boy, but it didn't extend much beyond that moment for me. Even though it seemed as though all my classmates were involved in hunting to some capacity, it didn't hold my interest in the least for several more years.

From that point, I was the typical "momma's boy." I did everything with my mother and rarely left her side because I just didn't enjoy the outdoors like most. My intellect caused my disposition to be towards the indoors and my lack of athleticism kept me there. Books became my life until I turned of age where most of my friends were driving. These mobile friends aspired to do little more than hunt or fish all day, every day. It didn't seem as though there were a lot of another choice in the South. Along with these friendships came my second attempt at the world of hunting.

It didn't take long before hunting began to allow my competitive side to shine. Some may say that I was a natural, but it's apparent that God's abundant favor always overshadowed my life and hunting was no exemption. I quickly learned that hunting was as much about ego as it was about the harvest. My friends bragged on who shot the biggest buck, how far away it was standing when they shot, who harvested the most deer/turkey that season, and eventually the type of equipment they used began to play a more prominent role in their stories.

Although firearms were in my mind the easiest method to ensure a harvest, I was instantly drawn to the realm of archery. I honed my archery skills through competition. However, I quickly learned that hunting deer took much more than learning how to make a good shot. There was much more involved in preparation for the hunt and the process after placing a shot than I could have imagined at first. The hunter must be adept with many tools to be able to successfully bring home a harvest.

Next, I learned about Arkansas' Triple Trophy Award program in which a hunter being skilled in multiple areas received an award for the successful harvest of three deer with at least one taken by each weapon of archery, muzzleloading, and modern weapon (shotgun, rifle, etc.). It was during the years that I strove for this new achievement that I realized both the complexity and benefit of being one individual qualified to handle multiple tools and weapons. I found that not every weapon is a good fit for every season or location; this is a skill set the church could vastly benefit from implementing.

Overview

In the letter to the church at Ephesus, Paul instructs the local gathering that Christ gifted the body with five ministerial positions. The offices that Paul listed are often referred to as the 'Five Fold Ministry' and are more specifically: apostle, prophet, evangelist, shepherd, and teacher. Each one of these offices was gifted by Christ not just for the early church but for the church to become all he created it to be.

Ephesians 4:11 - And he gave the apostles, the prophets, the evangelists, the shepherds and teachers,

If any one of these offices are lacking within the global Church or absent within the local church then we are not becoming that which Christ commissioned us. I like to think of it akin to the Triple Trophy Award. If we want to receive our heavenly reward for ministry here on earth, then if takes multiple types of weapons being involved in the harvest. Christ gifted all five positions to the church knowing that no singular office would be enough and that without all five not every person could be met with the gospel. Not every weapon fits every season or location; not every ministerial office can reach everyone. Yet everyone cannot be reached without all five being active in the role of ministry.

Paul tells us that Christ gifted the Five Fold to the church. It is pertinent for us to first understand that as the Holy Spirit gifts believers with various manifestations of his presence; those graces are the gifts. However, in regards to the Five Fold, the individuals holding their respective offices are the gift to the church.

Apostle

The apostle and prophet in my previous analogy could easily be equated to the iconic archery equipment of bow and arrow. While many believe these to be archaic and irrelevant to the modern world, their significance cannot be overlooked by the established church. These two were ordained by God to gaze upon the heavenly blueprint and infiltrate the enemy's camp on earth to establish a culture that is the perfect rendition of the utopia they find in heaven.

The title apostle is found seventy-six times throughout the New Testament. Apostles are sent to lead.

Mark 3:14 - And he appointed twelve (whom he also named apostles) so that they might be with him and he might send them out to preach

The Greek word that is translated as apostles has its roots in secular origins. The original term apostle is a seafaring term referring to a captain of many boats. As ships set sail, there was one captain who oversaw the coordination of all boats on the same journey. This captain of captains was the apostle.

In the New Testament the apostles of the church were originally called as disciples to become fishers of men (Matthew 4:19) and were left as apostles (Matthew 10:2; Acts 1:2,25), trained to lead others to make disciples who are fishers of men. In similar fashion to the apostle-captain, apostles within the church are a "pastor of pastors."

Apostles focus on building God's kingdom here on earth. Their primary focus is on bringing heaven to earth and raising up other pastors and leaders to steward a conducive environment. They may at times function in any of the offices found in Ephesians 2:20 as they must be able to operate in any office in order to teach others how to successfully fulfill their position. Because of this unique capability of the apostle, the apostle is called to lead the five fold ministry and focuses their ministry on pastoring the other five fold ministers.

Prophet

The title prophet is found one hundred fifty-two times within the New Testament alone. Prophets are often known as seers; their ministry is two-fold. Prophets minister via foretelling and/or forthtelling. Due to the nature of their ministry, prophets have a special grace to intercede for the church.

Fortelling is the more renown working of a prophet. When a prophet foretells, God has given them a description of a future occurrence that will happen or is destined to happen without repentance. This is often given so that the body of believers knows that God will be with them to fulfill his promises or will not break covenant with them despite their sins.

Acts 3:23 - And it shall be that every soul who does not listen to that prophet shall be destroyed from the people.'

Forthelling, while not always as recognized as fortelling, is perhaps the more relevant work of the prophet. Forthtelling is the capability of the prophet to explain to the church how they are in relation to God's standard and what affect this will have on their lives. This work of the ministry is often compared to a builder's plumb line. A plumb line is a weight tied to a string which an architect would nail to a board raised from the foundation. As gravity causes the weight to fall directly to the ground, the string becomes a level by which the carpenter can assure his board is perfectly straight or plumb. In this analogy, the weight is the word of God, the line is the prophet, and the board being added to the construction is the church. Forthtelling can often be overlapped or overshadowed by foretelling.

Not everyone who prophesies, though, is a prophet. Prophecy is unique from the other ministerial offices in the fact that the gift of prophecy is also found in all three lists of spiritual gifts (motivational, manifestational, and ministerial) as well as is taught to be the one gift that each believer should seek after in being the greatest gift.

Prophecy should be rampant within the church, but prophets are not. Someone called to the office of the prophet is given a commission by God not to minister just to individuals but to minister to the local church in which they are ordained or at times to minister to the whole Church.

Teacher

The title teacher is found sixty-two times in the New Testament. Out of all five fold ministry positions, it is the most widely accepted within our culture. Teachers play a practical role in connecting the other ministry offices and discipling believers.

I would associate teachers in my hunting story to the muzzleloader. Teachers tend to bridge the gap between what most view as ancient ministerial offices and the newer positions of shepherd and evangelist.

Matthew 10:24 - "A disciple is not above his teacher, nor a servant above his master.

Teachers, while primarily responsible for creating materials to instruct the body on the ways of God, become a pivotal conjunction between apostle/prophet and shepherd/evangelist. Due to their function as a connector, I have chosen to list them here as opposed to the order found in Scripture.

Apostle/prophet are by nature focused on what heaven is doing, while shepherd/evangelist spend their time with practically meeting the tangible needs of the physical realm. Just as the soul connects the spirit to the flesh, teachers have the uncanny ability of connecting the spiritual ministers to the physical ministers.

Teachers, however, face a unique challenge. Being the most widely accepted office as a whole has its benefits, yet teachers must truly distinguish their ministerial role as their title has become extremely secularized. Often times when we think of teachers, our thoughts go towards institutions of learning: K-12, colleges, universities, and even seminaries. This secular paradigm can manipulate the office of teacher to allow their goal to be to win a debate rather than to seek the truth in love.

Shepherd

The title shepherd is found twenty-two times in the New Testament. All shepherds are pastors; not all pastors are shepherds. The title pastor is not found anywhere in the New Testament according to the English Standard Version. This more modern translation has abandoned the title pastor in part to the previous statement. It has become widely accepted within our culture that the term pastor is synonymous to one who is leading a local church. However, that is not always the case.

For instance, Timothy is told that while he is pastoring he must do the work of an evangelist. While western tradition views Timothy as a pastor who is told not to forget to evangelize, Eastern Orthodox believers have unlocked a vital truth: Timothy was an evangelist who was being instructed by his apostles to not let his current season and position cause him to not fulfill the call of God on his life to be an evangelist. The church at

Ephesus for a season had an evangelist as their pastor, but that didn't make Timothy a shepherd.

The term pastor then should be viewed as a title for all ministers when someone simply is unaware of the proper title to crown them with. This could be compared to how Miss was once an acceptable title for any woman until one became aware of their marital status. In our local church, our leadership has the understanding that our culture is not one which widely accepts the five fold offices as of yet. Therefore within our staff we are aware of the different offices and functions each of us hold: we are divinely divided. However, to the church we are all pastors: united as one. In our unique case, the title pastor is a unifying term. It's crucial to understand, though, that we strive to have all five ministerial offices filled and functioning within our leadership. Without all five the church cannot be what it was created to be. Not all pastors are shepherds at our church; all shepherds, however, are all pastors.

The biblical title shepherd is a unique style of leadership. Shepherds by nature are very focused on the members of the household of God, often times referred to in the Bible as sheep. Shepherds tend to lead from the back. They are very gracious in their leadership style and allow believers to move forward according to their own will while monitoring their direction. Shepherds lead from the rear so that they may monitor the entire flocks movement to ensure that not even one strays from the straight and narrow path.

We must encourage shepherds not to be overly empathetic. While they are primarily responsible for feeding the sheep, Jesus also asked Peter to tend the sheep.

John 21:16 - He said to him a second time, "Simon, son of John, do you love me?" He said to him, "Yes, Lord; you know that I love you." He said to him, "Tend my sheep."

To tend a sheep means to protect the sheep. A shepherd must be willing to lay down his spiritual and at times even physical life for the wellbeing of the sheep. Often times shepherds will be pulled out of the time of isolation with God to minister to a believer.

To tend the sheep means to discipline the sheep as well. Church government, especially discipline, is one of the most misunderstood aspects of ministry. We must have an equal understanding that shepherds would often times take their staff and break the leg of a sheep that continued to wander and refused gentle correction. The shepherd would then carry this sheep while the leg healed teaching the sheep the importance of being close to the heart of the shepherd.

Evangelist

While listed among the five fold offices, the title of evangelist is only found two other places in the New Testament. Following shepherds, evangelists are among the most widely accepted ministry office within the modern church. Philip is the only undisputable evangelist we see in Scripture.

Acts 21:8 - On the next day we departed and came to Caesarea, and we entered the house of Philip the evangelist, who was one of the seven, and stayed with him.

Evangelists are like handguns. A lot of people have them, but few are trained how to use them. Evangelist focus the bulk of their ministry on reaching the lost. They hold the position specifically tasked for the unchurched. Evangelists have a special ability of sharing the good news in such a way to introduce a real relationship with God for the first time or to bring someone back to Jesus.

It is ironic that shepherds and evangelists are the most common positions held in the modern church considering they are the two positions least spoken about in Scripture. Teachers, shepherds, and evangelists combined are discussed far less in Scripture than apostles and prophets combined. Honestly, the church has almost no biblical standard for the office of evangelist.

However, we know it is critical to the church's mission as Paul lists it among the five offices in which Christ gifted the church. The church, though, shouldn't more readily accept a job description we've created than ones we clearly have received by God. It causes me to ponder if the church has adopted a mentality that, "I can do a better job of living up to my own expectations of life and ministry than what is clearly presented in the Bible by the authors."

Regardless to their rarity in Scripture versus the reality in which we live in modern times, evangelists are among the five offices and the church is dependent upon their role in ministry.

Without an evangelist being present and active, the church would become stagnant and incapable of spreading the gospel to the ends of the earth. An unfocused balance on any of the five offices causes the church to become hyper-focused and unable to fulfill its mission.

Heavenly Funnel

The collaboration of the five fold ministers create a heavenly funnel. If all five offices are fulfilling their function within a healthy church, a funnel from heaven is created for that local church body. To better describe this, imagine an hourglass that is nestled between heaven and earth. Apostles and prophets minister from the heavenly places according to their callings. Shepherds and evangelists minister to the needs of the people here on earth. Teachers become the small connector to ensure that what the apostles and prophets gather from heaven is funneled to the shepherds and evangelists where they may release it to the people. This by no means suggests that the first three ministers do not directly relate to people; it is a depiction of the necessity of each office's function in the mandate to release heaven on earth.

The only way the five offices operate effectively for the church is if they are in unison and understand functional subordination. Although no one office is in direct superiority to another (they are all as equally important in ensuring the church receives full ministering and equipping), the ministers must master functional subordination. Functional subordination acknowledges that while all offices are of equal importance, one must come under submission to another to maintain a proper flow.

-Functional Subordination

We see functional subordination demonstrated in the Godhead particularly in the life of Jesus here on earth. Jesus says that he did nothing without first seeing the Father do it. Consequently, while he could have released heaven to earth under his own authority, Jesus did not perform any miracles until the Holy Spirit came upon him and empowered him through the gifts. Jesus is by no means less God than either Father or Spirit, yet during his life and ministry Jesus maintained functional subordination to them both. Functional subordination was how Jesus maintained and released the gospel to the earth.

In Paul's description of the five fold ministers, he says that apostles and prophets make up the foundation while Christ is the cornerstone in which they build. Apostles build and prophets steady the foundation by making certain that new growth is in line with the cornerstone. Teachers then create a framework by which shepherds develop an atmosphere of comfort within the house of God. Evangelists, of course, invite in new guests. This depiction is very fitting for Christ's 'upside-down kingdom.'

The reality is that even though apostles and prophets are depicted as the lowest position and the servant of all as they expand the foundation, they hold the highest authority in the church. The proper order of functional subordination for the five ministers is: apostle > prophet > teacher >

shepherd > evangelist. This is why I chose to list the teacher out of order from the original listing. It is only when these five submit to one another's office in this order and maintain the honor of the office that God release his blessings through them into the body. This is why Paul describes the individuals who hold these offices as the gifts to the church themselves. While God is able to pour out his mercy, gifts, and blessings from heaven; the church is able to maintain those gifts with upright character.

<u>-Five Minister's Ministering</u>

Each of the five fold ministers have a divine role in the work of ministry. When all five offices are fulfilling their calling, the church is becoming all it was created to be. Apostles expand the house of God; they build what has been authorized by God. Apostles birth new ministries and empower other leaders to do the same. Prophets see what is being built and keep it in alignment with both the Bible and what God is doing in that season for the corporate church. Teachers provide resources to document what has been done and give a scriptural basis for believers. They also establish and maintain the doctrines and core beliefs of the body. Shepherds meet the tangible needs of the body. They provide comfort and stability within the local church. Evangelists invite new participants to join what God is doing locally.

When all five offices work together, we see: apostles launching new churches and ministries that are aligned with the prophets biblical vision of what God is doing in that time; evangelists bringing in new members to these new ministries and shepherds creating an environment conducive to learning; teachers then disciple these converts into Christians, they are taught all that Christ taught and to seek the higher gifts whereby birthing more apostolic and prophetic ministries.

Purpose of Ministers

Each of the five fold ministers serve a purpose individually, but more importantly they serve the purpose collectively. Their primary purpose is to equip the saints for the work of the ministry and to build up the body of Christ. These divine divisions in leadership create unity in the body. They create a heavenly funnel for every believer to become mature in Christ and to appear more Christ-like in their daily lives. When each office is working properly, the body is working properly: it is capable of growing itself in love.

Without these five offices functioning in the local church, our gatherings will never be all that Christ intended for them to be. Without all five, believers are not fully instructed as to how to grow their personal relationship and ministries. Without the five, the church grows in numbers without maturity. We then saturate our churches with selfish children who are more concerned with being identified by God than on working as a unified church. Believers who are considered to be mature are even carried from one local gathering to the next by what they think is the most up-to-date doctrine or the most captivating message of the moment. We settle for the goal of bringing everyone to God but fail to present a mature bride to Christ.

Together, the five offices of ministers create the weapon that the enemy cannot overcome: Christ's love, his church.

Chapter 3:
Demonic Four Fold

Before I begin this chapter, there are a few statements that must be made. If you don't believe in demons, it's most likely because you're oppressed by them. My belief comes from how prevalent the demonic was in Jesus' ministry, let alone the Bible as a whole. I once heard it said, 'If you aren't running into a demon every now and again as a Christian, you have to wonder if you're going in the right direction.' Walking upstream has a lot of resistance. I've also had my fair share of demonic encounters in a short tenure as a Christian.

The first time I encountered a demon possessed man I was barely a year old Christian. I was doing an internship in Nicaragua with a missionary organization. As I spent thirty days in this 'third world' country with few of the amenities I was used to, God began to challenge my soul on the deeper aspects of our relationship. Someone who is now a dear friend of mine began to share with me the concept of spiritual warfare. He taught me how to use my senses to discern the spiritual atmosphere in my vicinity. Then, he questioned my understanding of the spiritual gifts, particularly that of tongues. We came to a mutual understanding that if it was of God and would draw us closer to a relationship with him then we desired it; knowing God is good and all perfect gifts come from him and that he would not give his child something to harm him.

A few days later, I encountered more than a man at an evangelism crusade. As the worship team exited the stage and the evangelist began to share the gospel, I began to hear in the distance a tambourine. At first, I didn't pay much attention to this noise. After all, I had seen Nicaraguans bring a cowbell into worship previously. Then, I began to notice the regularity of the familiar chime. Every time the name of Jesus was mentioned the man would beat the tambourine, and he began to add something new. He was shouting. This was not an affirmative yes and amen either. Every time the evangelist shared about God's love through his son Jesus the man was using all his might and this instrument to detract and distract from the gospel presentation. He had to be confronted.

My new friend and I, along with another intern and translator, went over to confront the man. As we began to ask questions to him, the translator became a bridge for communication. That is, until she got a puzzled look on her face. The man's tone and rhythm shifted drastically; I already knew in my spirit what was taking place. The translators uncertain remark was only a validation. "I don't know what he is saying anymore," the translator shared hesitantly. My response, "I do." Although I had no clue what words were being said and had never been exposed to spiritual warfare, my spirit knew the intent. I fell on my knees knowing I didn't know what to say but that something needed to be proclaimed. It was in that moment that I prayed in tongues for the first time.

I don't really remember much else about that night. Honestly, I know the man left, but I cannot recall any more. During the altar call, the evangelist came to me and informed me he knew I had been seeking the gift of tongues. He questioned if I wanted more of God in my life. As the natural response was of course, I didn't even get to share my experience before he laid hands on me. I knew I had already received what he so desperately desired to impart to me that night. Sometimes ministers confer a gift; other times they confirm them.

Of course, this hasn't been my only encounter with the demonic in my life. The most intense attack was a direct attack against my life. I had still struggled for the next year about the relevance of the gifts of the Spirit. That struggle came to an abrupt halt when a demonic presence showed up in my room after having food poisoning. The enemy will always kick us when we're down. I still remember to this day what that demon's plan for my life was that night. Thankfully, not all demonic encounters have been against me personally. I've also seen demons manifest and throw individuals into seizures as they heard the name of Jesus. While these personal encounters are often the most vivid, I soon learned they aren't the most dangerous.

Demonic Authority

Demons operate under spiritual authority in a similar paradigm to believers. Think on that for a moment. When Satan rebelled against God, it was not only he who was cast out of heaven. What we learn from Scripture is that Satan was a high ranking angel; he spent much of his time in the direct presence of God. Because of his authority, it made it easy for him to convince many lower ranking angels to join him in his rebellion. His ploy was so successful that one out of every three angels joined Satan's civil war and were ultimately cast from heaven.

In the book of Ephesians, not only does Paul present to us the heavenly funnel, but he also informs us on the demonic hierarchy. We find this demonic hierarchy listed towards the end of the book in the infamous armor of God section.

Ephesians 6:12 - For we do not wrestle against flesh and blood, but against the rulers, against the authorities, against the cosmic powers over this present darkness, against the spiritual forces of evil in the heavenly places.

This demonic hierarchy is often times overlooked. However, as Paul instructs that this battle is not flesh in blood, we must conclude that not every enemy serves as a foot soldier.

As we study further into the various descriptions of demons that Paul gives us, we find several interesting facts. First, not every demon has the same authority or strategy against your life. Second, Paul lists these ranks in ascending order verifying their intensity as well as submission to

authority. Third, the demonic hierarchy is in direct
opposition to the five fold ministers.

Demonic Drain

Paul clarifies that the five fold ministry is a
heavenly funnel by giving us the depiction of
heaven before earth. The demonic drain is the
direct opposition. Demonic attack begins with an
earthly, fleshly basis and then grows into the
heavenly places as authority increases.

In the Great Commission, Jesus makes it
clear that all authority on heaven and earth is his.
He re-gifts authority to believers. Mankind had
authority, but chose to give it away when Adam
sinned in the Garden of Eden. During his
commissioning, Jesus restores authority to
believers. Satan knows that his authority has been
permanently removed and the only hope of
receiving authority now is to steal it from a believer.

Demons attempt to get believers to tolerate
sin which opens the door for demonic activity in
their life. As an individual refuses to deal with sin
within their heart, it becomes manifest sin within the
hands of their children. This is how generational
sins and curses begin. Then, sin continues to gain
empowerment as families grow and enlarge their
territory. The demons empowering this sin lifestyle
now gain regional authority. Families become
people groups, then nations. Before long, one sin
not dealt with can have influence over the world
with all demonic influencers alongside it.

Think of it this way, any sin that Noah took
with him off of the ark automatically influenced his
family. Had all family members chosen to walk in

this as well, the sin (and demonic) would continue to have an influence as they repopulated the world. What once only had a small influence gains by time and lack of repentance great influence. Satan continues to use this ploy today while focusing even more effort on the lives of believers. Demons acknowledge they have the rest of chronological time to gain authority and steal individuals from a relationship with God. This is how the demonic drain works.

Rulers

Rulers are the lowest rank in demonic authority. Rulers could also be translated as beginning and they are known as personal temptors. By every sense of the imagination, rulers are the little devil in the red outfit that sits on the left shoulder and whispers lies and temptations into our ear while Holy Spirit beckons truth from the other side. Perhaps, they aren't dressed as stereotypical with pitchfork in hand, but this perfectly illustrates their role.

From the perspective of warfare, most believers spend a majority of their time battling with rulers. These demons distract believers from any serious engagement in the spiritual war by maintaining focus on their personal life. Rulers are responsible for all those small fleeting thoughts that aren't godly. For instance, upon salvation Jesus states that we are born again, a new creation. From our rebirth, everything about us aligns with the will of God. I like to give it this illustration:
There once was an apple tree that began to experience rot. God knew that rotten fruit would do

no good so he removed this tree from his garden. Next, God planted an orange tree in its place. Now, this tree produces oranges; there is nothing within this tree that has the capability of producing apples even though apples were once produced from this location. The only way an apple can now get on this orange tree is if someone places an apple there to deceive those who walk by into thinking this may be an apple tree. *(Can a fig tree, my brothers, bear olives, or a grapevine produce figs? Neither can a salt pond yield fresh water. - James 3:12)*

Thoughts that do not align with God's will after salvation are demonic in nature. A majority of the time these thoughts are brought about by a personal ruler. Upon salvation, there is no longer anything within us capable of producing a sin thought. The only way those thoughts can now get there is if an outside influencer brings those thoughts in and with deception gets us to grant that way of thinking authority over our lives once again.

Authorities

Authorities are rulers with just a little bit more, well, authority. Authorities have spiritual influence over families and small territories. Once sin and demons aren't dealt with by parents, by nature every child they have will have to battle them at some point.

My Pastor used to say, "It's time to quit dealing with your Mommy's and Daddy's demons. If you really want demons to have influence over your life, there are enough out there to pick your own." His remark is a very real reminder to us all that demons crave being empowered over mankind and we cannot tolerate that.

Authorities are the scriptural term for generational demons. These demons no longer focus on tempting one individual. The scope of their influence is now an entire bloodline. They work in conjunction with all the rulers under them to get an entire family to commit to this sin and gain even more influence as that family does. Authorities are responsible for generational curses and generational sins.

It's important to add here that as we are not discussing a battle against flesh and blood we cannot solely limit demonic impression to physical families either. Demons would much rather gain traction among spiritual families. Sin that isn't dealt with within the minister's heart will become an authority over the life of his disciples. Demons strive to make divisions within the church and gain empowerment there as well.

Authorities also are the first level of the demonic to gain any sort of territorial dominion. The Greek word for authority can also be translated as jurisdiction. In the early days, authorities would have gained access by growth of an individual family. However, they may also gain empowerment by multiple families within a localized area granting authority to a certain demonic way of life.

As I purchased my first piece of property, I not only prayed over the house, but that the land would not be influenced by any demonic entity that was allowed to dwell on our street by the other homeowners. It's imperative to know that these demons attempt to gain control over our lives by those physically closest to us.

Cosmic Powers

Cosmic powers are world rulers. They are the demonic entities over cities, states, and/or nations. Cautiously, I state they are political in nature. Cosmic powers are demons that have gained enough influence over multiple regions to influence large territories. At this level, we truly begin to see demonic power manifest as an entire region has granted them strength.

As multiple family units and regions tolerate and at this point condone sin, demons are promoted to new levels of influence. The reason cosmic powers politic is to find commonality among individuals who may never meet and do not do life together. Cosmic powers create atmospheres of comfort for people ensnared in their sin.

My state, for instance, is a statistical nightmare for cosmic powers in regards to finances. Arkansas is almost always at the worst end of the scale for statistics in areas such as poverty and teen pregnancy. Being raised in this state, it is not only viewed as normal but acceptable when these sins are adopted. Cosmic powers even play into the political arena by passing laws which make it easy for that sin to remain. These laws do not assist hurting individuals to get out of sin, but actually create a culture where the sin is nurtured.

It's important for us to understand that demons are legalistic. They work with the sons of disobedience to create more laws in an attempt to create more opportunities for humanity to fall short of God's standards. Demons know the Bible better than most believers; they've had it quoted at them for thousands of years. They are very intune with the fact that God created government to protect his church and that we are advised to obey the law of the land. Their solution: create laws which are contradictory to the purpose of the church.

Demons communicate. It's how they appear to have words of knowledge. Spirit travels faster than sound or light [God spoke and then there was light]. This is how people with similar sins or coexisting sins, such as an abuser and a woman who has been abused, always engage with one another in the same room. Cosmic powers are working with authorities and rulers to expand their influence.

The most notable story of a cosmic power in my mind is when Jesus encounters the Legion of demons. As soon as Jesus steps on the land, the Legion met Jesus there. After these demons drown the herd of pigs, the herdsmen testified in the city what had occurred. Here is where we see the demons advanced influence as a cosmic power:

Luke 8:37 - Then all the people of the surrounding country of the Gerasenes asked him to depart from them, for they were seized with great fear. So he got into the boat and returned.

All of the people agreed together that they did not want Jesus in their country if he was able to cast the spirits out of this man. The city had long accepted that this man would stay in his demonic lifestyle and even empowered the demons in his life by granting him to stay among the tombs. The man ultimately goes throughout the city declaring his gospel in an attempt to destroy the yoke in this city.

He had received the special grace by Jesus to destroy the cosmic power's influence in this region.

Spiritual Forces of Evil

Spiritual forces of evil in the heavenly places are the highest rank of demons. These are the demonic entities who wage war against God's archangels. Very few demons are granted enough power to have influence over cosmic powers, authorities, and rulers. These spirits command demon armies to wage war against the earth.

Spiritual forces of evil impact multiple nations, whole continents, or even the entire world. Spiritual forces are truly wicked. They no longer focus on physical sin as a doorway, but seek full oppression over the world spiritually.

Satan himself once served God in his inner courts before his rebellion. It has long been his goal to have that much authority given to him once again. His desire now is to not only stir a rebellion among the angels but also within the whole earth. The only way Satan, or any other demon, can be elevated to the heavenly places once again is by mass oppression throughout the earth.

Spiritual forces of evil are truly wicked because of the sheer volume of agreement they master of the demonic realm and the human mind. These demons have studied human behavior for long enough to know what sins are common throughout the world. It is not just that man has a propensity towards sin; sin nature is groomed by demons who are seated in heavenly places oppressing the globe.

We must understand a few facts in order to truly dethrone demons once again. First, Satan (and all other demons) at most are counterparts to Michael (and other archangels). God and Satan are not equal opposites. No amount of power gathered by all demons could ever dethrone God. The war is among the angelic and demonic over the souls of humans. Second, demons were removed from heaven by God. They have no right to be in heavenly places ever again, unless mankind grants them such power. Jesus declares before his ascension that all authority on heaven and earth is his. He shares with his followers that he is restoring authority to mankind through his church. At the point of salvation, we are seated with Christ in heavenly places.

Ephesians 2:6 - and raised us up with him and seated us with him in the heavenly places in Christ Jesus,

All believers have more authority than any and every demon. However, we need a strategy if we intend on removing their oppression.

Underview

The goal of the demonic drain is to hinder the performance of the five fold ministry. Demons spend their time with unbelievers doing all they can to shelter their minds from the revelation of the one true God. Once an individual has experienced salvation, it becomes the goal of every demon in association with that person to keep them in sin and broken fellowship with God. Ultimately for the church, though, demons desire to see an oppressed body that is disunified and immature.

The easiest way to begin combating demonic influence over our personal lives starts within our soul: mind, will, and emotions. We must recognize that not every thought that comes into our minds daily is one of our own. Once those thoughts are realized, the source of them can be dealt with.

Back to the orange tree illustration: the only way an apple can stay on an orange tree is if someone allows it to sit there. I once heard in reference to this teaching that a pastor quit repenting for thoughts that didn't align with scripture. Simply put, he stated that upon salvation he was born again which includes a new way of thinking perfectly in line with the will of God. Therefore, any thought contradictory to that must have originated outside him (it was placed there by a demon). As he, and then I, began to have thoughts come into our mind contrary to the will of God, we no longer spent time lamenting over how that thought could have gotten back into our lives and began dismissing those thoughts and dismantling the enemy.

On a grander scale for the church as a whole, though, not every believer is mature enough to or even exposed to the teaching to be aware of their thought life. We must then come to the conclusion that there must be believers who cover less mature believers and can deliver them from demonic oppression. This describes the five fold ministry.

<u>Five > Four</u>

The ministers that have the greatest spiritual influence over the enemy are of course the apostles and prophets as they lay the foundation for the church and spend the bulk of their ministry from what heaven is saying. Prophets, however, are not quite as equipped as apostles in regards to the demonic. Several times throughout scripture prophets act on God's behalf and disshovel the demons only to be thwarted and retreat in fear to counter attacks.

Apostles, on the other hand, have a natural expression of their anointing that expose demons. Without any thought or warning, demons are both attracted to and unveiled by the presence of an apostle. The apostolic is a vital role in the life of every believer and local church. Apostles are even more critical in obtaining and maintaining unity in the body as a whole.

Chapter 4:
Apostle's Role Defined

'You will be a Pastor of pastors. Very similar to the man you see ministering on the stage today, but different. There will be more, much more. God told me to tell you not to try to figure it out. Don't over-analyze it. Just believe it. [And receive it.]'

The first time I was prophesied over I didn't even know what prophecy was, much less what to do with it. Honestly, I was more interested in understanding the logic behind the various tongues I was hearing surrounding me. I was told by my mentor we were going to a prayer meeting, but I didn't know we were going to experience that. We hadn't even discussed tongues yet. I didn't know what I believed about them. Afterall, I just got saved at a Baptist Church. And what was up with those dance moves?

Needless to say, God told me not to figure it out, so I just stuck the prophetic word in the back pocket of my mind. I felt I was called to the ministry. I had to figure out how I would get in with a past like mine before I even thought about what it would look like.

Nevertheless, the prophetic word began to unfold over my life. The first time I went on a mission trip was to the country of Nicaragua. It was there I surrendered to ministry. The first week did not even pass before I began to weep knowing that I was called to serve God with all my life through the ministry.

I ended up going back to Nicaragua several more times. Throughout the evangelism crusades, vacation Bible schools, skits, and testimonies I began to notice one constant: there was one people group who always missed our ministry efforts. The least ministered to people group of all were the pastors. I began to feel convicted that I would soon travel to spend the next few years of my life in seminary surrounded by thousands of resources, many of which I would have electronically at my fingertips. Yet these men and women received little formal training or resources to assist their daily application of the gospel. These pastors were spiritually malnourished themselves. How could we expect them to make disciples full wisdom when they barely knew how to grow themselves? That's when it hit me: a congregation can only grow as high in their relationship with God as the leadership can take them.

That mantra became the foundation of my ministry. I asked the founder of the ministry there in Nicaragua if I could come back to teach all I learned in seminary. After my first year, my pastor and myself did exactly that. A few years later, I was invited back to another pastors' conference in Nicaragua by another ministry group.

However, my personal journey began to relocate me to develop my qualifications for pouring into other pastors. When I met my wife Natalie she had two thoughts about me pastoring pastors. First, she asserted that every good pastor needs a wife as that's the only way they can really disciple ladies and married couples. (While this logic holds true, I wonder if she was trying to rush my proposal. Haha.) Second, she questioned how well I could fulfill that calling if I had no experience pastoring myself. As we began to explore those thoughts, I surrendered to a newfound calling of church planting.

As I began to be trained for planting a church under the covering of my wife's home church, I began to notice something amazing about the congregation. The congregation of this local church included all walks of life, quite literally from prostitutes to preachers. I'm not even referring merely to the pastors on staff either. Several pastors came to this church to attend and be poured back into during times of healing or development.

When we planted the church, the same types of people began attending our church as well. At first, we had so many non-believers and new believers that no one even had experience taking up an offering. But then, we began to see pastors and lots of them. There were as many pastors in our church of fifty as in our sending church of a thousand. This wasn't a LifeBridge thing though, there was something about my pastor's leadership style and that of myself which drew pastors to be pastored.

Original Apostles

Mark 3:14 - And he appointed twelve (whom he also named apostles) so that they might be with him and he might send them out to preach

The Greek term which is translated as apostle is a unique choice made by Jesus to describe his twelve greatest disciples. Jesus chose a term that would best relate to the men he chose to birth his new covenant church on earth through. God would have it that this title for the highest office of ministry leadership would not be one easily recognized by the current church leadership nor even members. Jesus chose a secular term to describe the twelve apostles.

The original term apostles is a seafaring term. This seems a logical choice made by Jesus as a majority of the men he chose to hold this office had a background in fishing and all of them were at least exposed to that culture. The term apostle represents the highest rank among fisherman. As ships would set sail, captains determined their coordinates, but apostles command captains. This term would have been equivalent as a "captain of captains." Therefore, it's easy to see that Jesus could have easily made the simile to the term becoming a Pastor of pastors.

The uniqueness of this title is perhaps best found in Jesus' original calling of his disciples. As Jesus first calls Simon Peter and Andrew, he makes an unusual offer to them:

Matthew 4:19 - And he said to them, "Follow me, and I will make you fishers of men."

As Jesus finds these men, they are set with a steady occupation of fishing, perhaps not the most lucrative but certainly a consistent job. These men must choose to give up their entire way of living in hopes that following Jesus provides more than just eternal provision.

When Jesus leaves the eleven, his work is complete and theirs begins. No longer are they mere fishermen, but fishers of men. Jesus goes so far as to elevate them one more time: he informs them that they are not just to fish for men by themselves but are now captains who will disciple other captains in fishing for men. As Jesus launches the modern church, he commissions Peter and the other apostles to teach others to be like them: disciples who make disciples, captains who make fishers of men, apostles who grow other leaders to grow other leaders to continue the cycle and perpetually grow the church.

Modern Day Apostles

While some modern church cultures (i.e. denominations) like to think the apostles are long dead and gone, we cannot deny the validity of their role in ministry. Apostles hold a special ministry office which cannot be negated by the modern church. As previously stated (and it bears repeating), the church cannot be all that it was created to be without all of the five fold ministry. That statement is especially true in regards to apostles.

The role is ever more crucial in the church today. While apostles have several core values of their ministry, the underlying focus of all apostles is to replicate heaven on earth. As the captain-apostles led their teams of ships through uncharted waters, their role didn't end once they docked on dry land. Upon discovering new territory, the role of an apostle became making the culture of new territory look like the culture of kingdom

Matthew 10:5-8 - These twelve Jesus sent out, instructing them, "Go nowhere among the Gentiles and enter no town of the Samaritans, but go rather to the lost sheep of the house of Israel. And proclaim as you go, saying, 'The kingdom of heaven is at hand.' Heal the sick, raise the dead, cleanse lepers, cast out demons. You received without paying; give without pay.

Replicating the culture of the kingdom was especially important as the King's ultimate desire was for all his kingdom to have the same culture. King's also want to feel welcome when they entire regions of their territory they haven't been to previously or at least recently. A King desires unity and apostles ensure the territory they govern looks as much like their home as possible.

We see the apostolic commission in the Lord's model prayer.

Matthew 6:10 - Your kingdom come, your will be done, on earth as it is in heaven.

Jesus taught the original apostles to pray for God's will to be done on earth as it is currently being done and will forever be done in heaven. Knowing that Jesus informed the apostles for this to be a part of their prayer to Our Father, we must conclude that

God's desire is to see the same culture of heaven (worship, health, spiritual purity, provision, etc.) [and the same culture he started in the Garden of Eden] restored to all humanity.

The apostolic calling is a diplomatic calling. Just as Paul calls us to be ambassadors, the apostles take this to a new level in establishing embassies and duplicating the culture of the Kingdom. Modern apostles are the foundation of God reaching new people groups and areas in new ways while re-establishing his kingdom here on earth.

Leader of Leaders

Apostles are sent to lead. As with the original term, the biblical apostles are sent out by the King to be a leader of leaders. Apostles make disciples who make disciples who make disciples. They focus their ministry on equipping and empowering those called to leadership. Without healthy leadership, the church body will wither.

The Apostle is called primarily to lead the five fold ministry. However, the apostolic mandate is not absent of the leadership metrics set by Jesus.

Matthew 23:11 - The greatest among you shall be your servant.

In God's kingdom, to be able to lead is to be called to serve. To be able to lead someone in leadership, you've had to have gone before them. Because of this the apostle can, at any time, operate out of any of the other four offices.

Apostles can function in any of the offices listed in Ephesians 2:20. They are a "Pastor of pastors." Recall Timothy, who the Eastern Church recognizes as evangelist doing the work of the pastor or as the Western Church asserts the reverse. Either way, Timothy had the capability of serving in more than one of the five fold ministry offices.

The anointing of the Apostle contains a quality within the mantle that stimulates and draws to the surface the diverse anointings of the people around him/her. Apostles by nature draw future leaders to them who must be called forth and equipped. While all the five fold offices are charged with equipping the saints, apostles focus on those who will become the next generation's five fold leaders. Prophets can greatly assist apostles with this role as prophets often see a person's purpose over their situation and call them into the ministry.

Heavenly strategists

Apostles are heavenly strategists. The apostles see what heaven is doing and release that here on earth. As much as we learn from the twelve apostles, we must realize that Jesus is our ultimate guide to apostleship.

Hebrews 3:1 - Therefore, holy brothers, you who share in a heavenly calling, consider Jesus, the apostle and high priest of our confession,

Jesus, the apostle, came with the mission of establishing the kingdom of God here on earth again. He came with the message that God's

61

kingdom was at hand, literally within the fingertips of the people he was ministering to. Jesus' model prayer is an apostolic prayer. During it, Jesus prayed :

Matthew 6:10 - Your kingdom come, your will be done, on earth as it is in heaven.

This phrase was the mantra of Jesus' ministry and the heart of the apostolic: to release the kingdom of God on earth as it is currently being done and forever will be done in heaven.

Apostles focus on building God's kingdom here on earth. Their primary focus is on bringing heaven to earth and raising up other pastors and leaders to steward a conducive environment. Jesus wasn't merely focused on how much heaven he could release through himself; he spent a majority of his ministry raising up the next generation apostles who were equipped to do the same.

Paul, the apostle, depicts the heavenly strategist by the term master builder.

1 Corinthians 3:10 - According to the grace of God given to me, like a skilled master builder I laid a foundation, and someone else is building upon it. Let each one take care how he builds upon it.

Paul acknowledged that one of his chief roles as an apostle was to expand the foundation on which the church would be built. The Greek word which is translated here as master builder has the same root word which we derive the word architect. Apostles, including Paul, are master builders of heaven here on earth. Just as an architect is capable of looking at any blueprint to determine where they are in the construction process, so too apostles have a gifting to identify underlying faults in the build.

Due to the nature of being a heavenly strategist, apostles easily see what is absent in the local church. I recall in the early years of our marriage visiting several churches with Natalie as we searched for which local gathering would nurture our marriage and callings. Natalie quickly tired of our post-service conversations. I could in just a few minutes see deep underlying hurts and areas of weakness. Although the apostolic in my life had not been matured and was at times fueled by arrogance, the giftings of God are without repentance *(Romans 11:29)*. Nevertheless, the apostolic was needed in those churches. Very few times did I have a rapport with the local pastor to have those conversations with him. However, someone needed to. Apostles easily identify what is hindering heaven from manifesting in the local church.

With that said, the Pharisees did the same thing. The Pharisees focused their ministry on all the areas God's people fell short in their worship. It's a heart position. Don't be a false apostle. Perhaps the church today is most concerned with advancing the apostolic because of fear of the false apostles. Afterall, revelation clearly states that they will be around *(Revelation 2:2)*. Yet if false apostles will have influence, we must come to the conclusion that it is because the true apostolic calling will never leave the church prior to the return of Jesus.

For those called to the apostolic, we must have the ability, first and foremost, to discover what is missing: why is the church not experiencing the same pure relationship with God that we experience in heaven. Second, we must consistently connect to others in our season and those who have gone before us. This keeps our hearts pure and aligned with God's movement. Finally, we must elevate to the next level. Our own ministry must become increasingly more like heaven as does the ministries we have influence over.

Father

Apostles are spiritual fathers and they establish a family culture. When someone is born into the kingdom of God, there are people who deliver them into new life. Often times, we consider the individuals who disciple us to be our spiritual parents. Apostles take this to heart. With the apostolic, there is a high value for a spiritual family culture.

Apostles value covenant relationship over the benefits they can receive from people. Just as with our Heavenly Father, no amount of wrong can remove our identity as a child. The same holds true with a spiritual family. Apostles discipline like a father and maintain a relationship with children who are struggling to perform in this new life. As a spiritual father, apostles desire for their spiritual children to be propelled forward because of their spiritual heritage. Apostles desire more for their spiritual children than from them.

The same is true within the five fold ministry. Apostles tend to let leaders lead and only correct them when they stray too far off the path of the vision. Therefore, by nature, an apostolic culture values an atmosphere of creativity over conformity. New growth is developed where creativity is encouraged and mistakes are allowed.

This creates a unique dynamic in an apostolic family. In an apostolic culture it is "okay" to make mistakes. Apostles understand that the only way to truly experience love is by the choice of rejection or acceptance. Spiritual children are expected to maintain holiness, though perfection is not forced. With holiness as the ultimate goal, sin is not seen as something that breaks fellowship but as an identity issue which must be walked through in maturity. Discipline is not fear based, but instill principles with freedom of choice.

Matthew 5:48 - You therefore must be perfect, as your heavenly Father is perfect.

When reading scripture and the teachings of Jesus, we have the choice of two perspectives. Option one is to see verses such as the one above as a command. By viewing this as a commandment of Christ, we must conclude that failure to perform this commandment falls short of God's standard which is by definition sin. Therefore the conclusion of option one would be that a lack of perfection is sin and breaks relationship with God. The mindset that Jesus spoke commandments is a performance-based identity and perpetuates discipline as conformity.

So if Jesus didn't speak commandments, what did he speak? Option two is to view the new covenant teachings as promises. As Jesus died on the cross and restored our relationship with God, he formed a new covenant with humanity. Jesus fulfilled the standard and commandments. Now, therefore, scripture no longer is a standard that believers live towards. Scripture is now the starting point in which we live our lives from. If our lives do not measure up in any area to the promises we find in the Bible, then, it is not a sin issue but an identity issue. Take for example the above referenced verse again, "be perfect." If this was a promise by Jesus that as believers we are perfect because the DNA of our Father is perfect, then any failure to be perfect is not an issue within our nature but our identity. Therefore all believers have perfection within them and the goal of apostolic ministry is one of reconciliation *(2 Corinthians 5:18)*. God promises that we are perfect as his children; what is hindering us from receiving that here on earth?

Apologists

Apostles are excellent apologists. If the term apologist is unfamiliar at first, know it does not mean that apostles are really good at apologizing for mistakes. Apologists are those who are well versed in the study of apologetics. Apologetics simply means to defend one's beliefs. We find the core Greek word for apologetics in Peter's first letter.

1 Peter 3:15 - but in your hearts honor Christ the Lord as holy, always being prepared to make a defense to anyone who asks you for a reason for the hope that is in you; yet do it with gentleness and respect,

Apologetics, while not limited to apostles only, is a familiarity with scripture at a deep enough level to make a proper defense for those attacking its truths. During my time in seminary, I attended a debate between six biblical scholars on the subject matter of homosexuality, three opposed and three for it. Both sets of scholars were well versed in the Bible and made their arguments not on surface level mistranslations but from the original language. It was through this debate that I saw the importance of not only how to make a defense, but how to pull down the defenses of the enemy.

2 Corinthians 10:5 - We destroy arguments and every lofty opinion raised against the knowledge of God, and take every thought captive to obey Christ,

Apologists must understand not only their biblical worldview, but must come to a gentle and respectful understanding of why other people believe lies. In order to be able to destroy an argument, you first have to understand the heart of the person who owns that belief system. Once you understand their mindset and can empathize with them, perhaps then they will be open to hearing the truth. No one has been won to Christ by a heated argument.

Philippians 1:16 - Some indeed preach Christ from envy and rivalry, but others from good will. The latter do it out of love, knowing that I am put here for the defense of the gospel.

Apostles value defending the word of God; knowing it is the standard of living for all humanity, not just believers.

Supernatural

Apostles walk in the supernatural. Apostolic ministries are characterized by miracles and manifestations. As apostles steward the release of heaven to earth, the supernatural is revealed as God's natural order. During the process of releasing the spirituals (spiritual gifts), there is friction caused by the demonic. Angelic beings are exposed: both those serving the Lord and the fallen demonic entities.

In John chapter fourteen, Jesus promises that his disciples will do greater works than they experienced with him present because he is going to the Father to intercede on their behalf. Quickly after the baptism of the Holy Spirit in the book of Acts, we begin to see the apostles walk in this promise.

Acts 2:43 - And awe came upon every soul, and many wonders and signs were being done through the apostles.

Acts 5:12 - Now many signs and wonders were regularly done among the people by the hands of the apostles. And they were all together in Solomon's Portico.

The apostles began to move in the spiritual gifts in new ways they had not experienced even in the presence of Jesus. For instance, they saw people instantly healed under the shadow of Peter (*Acts 5:15*) and others healed simply because cloths the apostles touched were brought to them (*Acts 19:12*).

Many of the healings the apostles saw in the early church were physical, but several of them were spiritual as well. Apostles administer the miraculous and this causes demons to manifest.

Acts 16:16-17 - As we were going to the place of prayer, we were met by a slave girl who had a spirit of divination and brought her owners much gain by Fortune-telling. She followed Paul and us, crying out, "These men are servants of the Most High God, who proclaim to you the way of salvation."

Apostles walk in such a high spiritual authority that demons cannot sit in silence and watch them walk by. I have literally seen demons not be able to form sentences as they manifest through an individual in the presence of an apostle. I've even seen demons manifest over media and tell their name/assignment as apostle tunes in to watch. Demons are so irked by the apostolic ministry that they must make their presence known. This becomes a key in apostolic discernment and aids the church in fulfilling the call of God upon their lives.

[We examine this final feature more in chapters 6-10].

Chapter 5:
Diverse Apostolic Callings

Growing up my Dad owned a pre-owned car dealership. There were three other men who worked there alongside my dad and myself during the summers. I was taught through my experiences to value hard-work from the tires up. (Hopefully, I'm still trusted after sharing my background as a used car salesman. Haha.)

Nevertheless, growing up as an entrepreneur's son taught me many life skills and gave me a unique outlook on life. I noticed that each of the men, and even myself, were valuable assets to the car lots. At times, their job descriptions would overlap as the ultimate goal was the profitability of the business. Day to day, though, each one of us had our own function that matched our personality and background.

When I say I learned to value hard-work from the tires up, I make that statement because I began with the lowest rank position: car detailer. Of course, there is nothing wrong with this position, but no adolescent male wants to be scrubbing carpets when they could be collecting the payments. Yet bookkeeping was someone else's job. I spent a majority of my time in the shop alongside the man who was responsible for repairs and maintenance of the vehicles. Occasionally we would see the fourth guy whose focus was on sales as he brought us a car which needed 'tuned up' from the second lot. Finally, or better said first, was my Dad. He wasn't always there, but that was necessary. He traveled often to purchase the best value vehicles and often found himself in business meetings with bankers or accountants. We were a well disciplined crew who enjoyed being around one another and the tasks we were responsible for. I cannot tell you the countless times the mechanic came to my aid or how I saw all of them standing together under a hood.

As I grew older, each one of the others took time to teach me the skills they possessed and their functionality for the business. I learned that each one of them held a crucial role to the growth and maintenance of the business. Without even one of them being present, the business would fail. If cars weren't cleaned or in good working condition, no sales could be made. If cars were cleaned and operable, but no one sold them no payments could be collected. If the three of us were performing to the best of our capability, but not one ensured the purchasers actually paid there would be cash flow issues. If no one bought more vehicles or more importantly paid the bills, there would be no workers.

I see this same type of camaraderie among the original apostles. Every apostle that Jesus chose held the same mantle: apostle. Yet each one of the apostles fulfilled that calling in a unique way in which only that person was capable. The expression of apostleship is as different as the person. If any of the apostles chose not to follow Jesus, the church would be lacking in a vital way. All apostles advance the gospel and establish the kingdom of God here on earth, but no one does it exactly the same. From the people group to the method of discipleship, the original apostles set a standard for diversity among those who hold this office.

Peter

Peter holds the iconic role of apostle. Numbered as one of the original twelve apostles, Peter always stands out among the others because he was never ashamed to share what was on his mind. Peter wasn't just an apostle though, he was one of the three closest friendships that Jesus had on earth.

Peter is an Apostle Preacher. From the moment Holy Spirit's ministry was launched on the earth, Peter became a mouthpiece of leadership for the Lord.

Acts 2:14 - But Peter, standing with the eleven, lifted up his voice and addressed them: "Men of Judea and all who dwell in Jerusalem, let this be known to you, and give ear to my words.

Peter's ministry is most characterized by his preaching. Throughout the book of Acts, Peter repetitively stands up and preaches the gospel. In the couple of letters written by Peter, he doesn't recount the life of Jesus or focus on clarifying church doctrines, he focuses penning the gospel and the role of the believer in its advancement.

Apostle preachers are scattered throughout the pulpits in modern times as well. Not everyone who stands up to preach the gospel is a shepherd 'pastor' as culture often dictates. Many who preach hold a different office and apostle preachers have the unique characteristic of bringing forth apostolic vision through preaching.

Acts 4:13 - Now when they saw the boldness of Peter and John, and perceived that they were uneducated, common men, they were astonished. And they recognized that they had been with Jesus.

Apostle preachers bring forth what they see being done in the heavenlies with a strategy to release that here on earth through the local church.

Peter, however, holds another unique apostolic characteristic. Peter wasn't just an Apostle Preacher. Peter was an Apostles' Apostle. After Jesus' ministry was completed, the other ten still needed someone to guide them in their apostolic mandate. Peter took on the responsibility of the highest authoritative position.

Acts 1:15 - In those days Peter stood up among the brothers (the company of persons was in all about 120) and said,

From that moment, it became apparent that Peter was to be the Apostles' Apostle. Even leaders need leadership. We see that all other ministry callings have the apostle to submit to spiritually for guidance and protection. But who do apostles submit to on earth? Of course their ultimate submission is to Jesus, yet apostles still need accountability and encouragement. That is the role of the Apostles' Apostle, an apostle to other apostles.

<u>Matthew</u>

Matthew was one of only two of the apostles to record the life of Jesus. Matthew's biography of Jesus was directed towards the Jewish community. With his background in accounting and tax collection, Matthew gives an excellent account of the fulfillment of the Law and Prophets through the life of Jesus.

Matthew 1:17 - So all the generations from Abraham to David were fourteen generations, and from David to the deportation to Babylon fourteen generations, and from the deportation to Babylon to the Christ fourteen generations.

Matthew was a Chronicler. His unique apostolic characteristic was to record the life of Jesus in such a way where Jews could easily correlate his life to the messianic promises. Matthew meticulously outlines the life of Jesus as the fulfillment of the messianic prophecies.

Chroniclers are those who record historical events. The first book of Chronicles has a remarkably similar introduction as the gospel of Matthew. Nearly the entirety of the first nine chapters of First Chronicles are devoted to genealogies. Historically, it was crucial for the Jewish community to prove their lineage to the promises of God. Chroniclers recorded the necessary history to recount the movements of God in relation to the Jewish people.

Matthew follows a similar pattern for his genealogy of Jesus. He begins his gospel recollection with this trait so that the Jews would have no doubt of Jesus' ability to make the claim of Messiah. As a chronicler, Matthew would have the unique writing style of connecting the history of God's people to the modern movement of God.

Matthew's gospel is a great rendition of when the apostolic meets the natural. As a chronicler, Matthew would have been able to record the life of Jesus. As an apostle, Matthew was able to acknowledge more than just historical Jesus. Matthew records the fulfillment of the Law and Prophets by Jesus, yet he does so in such a way where his focus is on what heaven is bringing to earth. Matthew records several unique stories in his gospel such as the Sermon on the Mount, the Lord's Prayer, and the Great Commission. These three alone reveal the apostolic nature of Matthew's chronicling. Matthew was able to see what would be needed by the future church to fulfill the call to follow Jesus.

Keep in mind, Matthew was the one to record the greatest apostolic prayer of Jesus:

Matthew 6:9-13 - Pray then like this: "Our Father in heaven, hallowed be your name. Your kingdom come, your will be done, on earth as it is in heaven. Give us this day our daily bread, and forgive us our debts, as we also have forgiven our debtors. And lead us not into temptation, but deliver us from evil.

Paul

Paul was an Apostle Author. All of the contributors of the New Testament wrote, but Paul had a scribe anointing. Paul penned half of the New Testament literature. Paul's character shines through his writing. Paul wrote with both fluency and captivity.

However, Paul was not a very articulate speaker.

2 Corinthians 10:10 - For they say, "His letters are weighty and strong, but his bodily presence is weak, and his speech of no account."

Paul was very long-winded in his speaking. In fact, Paul was such an uncaptivating presenter that his sermon killed a man.

Acts 20:9 - And a young man named Eutychus, sitting at the window, sank into a deep sleep as Paul talked still longer. And being overcome by sleep, he fell down from the third story and was taken up dead.

Luke recounts that Paul prolonged his speech until midnight causing this young man named Eutychus to fall asleep during the middle of the message. Of course Apostle Paul was able to restore life to the young man.

Paul, while not the most gifted preaching Apostle, was the most gifted writer. He wrote more quantitatively than any other contributor of the New Testament and his content is the backbone for most church doctrine in modern times. Paul's letters were always addressed to either specific local churches or their pastors. He used his background as a former Pharisee to connect the doctrines of Christianity to their Jewish roots.

Perhaps Paul was such a developed writer because of his consistency of praying in tongues.

1 Corinthians 14:18 - I thank God that I speak in tongues more than all of you.

It seems from the experience of Paul that in order to write the heart of God for future generations one should spend more alone time with God than apart from him. Speaking in tongues is critical to the exhortation of our spirit, but more is found in this gifting than that aspect alone. I like to think that much of Paul's revelation came from his speaking in tongues. If the Spirit is capable of speaking a corporate tongue which becomes prophecy during interpretation, who are we to limit that act only to spoken word? I believe Paul's writings (as all of Scripture) to be God-breathed and both inspired and infallible in the writing's original form. I submit though that Paul's unique ability to be the author of so much of the New Testament was directly tied to how often he prayed in tongues. (Even if that is not the case, would our writing/preaching be hindered by attempting to speak in tongues more? I'm assured the answer is no.)

John

The apostle John was extremely prophetic. John was a visionary as well as a seer. His ministry was characterized by apostolic vision, yet John also had perhaps the most intense prophetic vision in all of the Bible.

Proverbs 29:18 - Where there is no prophetic vision the people cast off restraint, but blessed is he who keeps the law.

The writings of John are unlike any other New Testament contributor. John was a prophetic author. We see the stark contrast of John's ministry beginning with the four gospels. Matthew, Mark, and Luke had a similar writing style. These three gospels compile what scholars refer to as the synoptic gospels. The synoptic gospels follow the same chronological outline and writing format. However, the gospel as recorded by John is much different. While the synoptic gospels are focused on recounting the life of Jesus chronologically, John's gospel recollection is both thematic and theological. John was much more focused on why God was creating a new covenant through Jesus than how.

John's apostolic ministry took on a whole new level during his time of exile on Patmos island. During his stay, John has delivered by an angel of the Lord a prophetic word for the church.

Revelation 1:1 - The revelation of Jesus Christ, which God gave him to show to his servants the things that must soon take place. He made it known by sending his angel to his servant John,

John's vision was both for the seven churches addressed in the letter as well as the Church in the end times. As the gospel writers recounted the life of Jesus and Luke collected the acts of the early apostles, Paul contributes the doctrines for the church to live by, and John at the end of the Scripture cannon releases a prophetic word by which the church must consistently measure itself until the return of Jesus.

Revelation 22:16 - "I, Jesus, have sent my angel to testify to you about these things for the churches. I am the root and the descendant of David, the bright morning star."

John moved as equally in the gifts of prophecy as his mantle of the apostolic. The unique character that John portrayed of functioning in both so fluently is greatly needed in the church in modern times. Yet let us constantly be aware that not all apostles will move as John ministered. Perhaps the following prophetic insight given by John is best suited for the modern church leadership to meditate upon:

Revelation 2:2 - "'I know your works, your toil and your patient endurance, and how you cannot bear with those who are evil, but have tested those who call themselves apostles and are not, and found them to be false.

As the church so desperately needs the apostolic to be restored in this hour, let us not recklessly abandon the truth in hopes of reconciliation.

Judas

Judas was an apostle. For brevity I have not included the entire passage, but these few verses within context prove that Judas was called an apostle by Jesus.

Acts 1:16-17 - "Brothers, the Scripture had to be fulfilled, which the Holy Spirit spoke beforehand by the mouth of David concerning <u>Judas</u>, who became a guide to those who arrested Jesus. For he was <u>numbered among us</u> and was allotted his share in this ministry." (underlining added for emphasis)

Acts 1:26 - And they cast lots for them, and the lot fell on Matthias, and he was <u>numbered with the eleven apostles</u>. (underlining added for emphasis)

Matthias replaced Judas' role as an apostle in the early church. Peter shared with the company of approximately one hundred twenty which gathered in the upper room that Pentecost Sunday that Judas' replacement was necessary to fulfill what was written about in the Psalms.

The key to understanding this passage is to understand who Judas Iscariot was. Judas was not just the betrayer of Jesus. For the entire three year apostolic seminary training that Jesus took the apostles on Judas was there and was numbered by Jesus as an apostle. Judas would have been present for all the signs, miracles, and wonders that took place not just through the hands of Jesus, but also the hands of the apostles. Judas, I believe, also walked in the miraculous. His personal ministry efforts could not be distinguished from the other apostles prior to his betrayal.

Matthew 7:21-23 - "Not everyone who says to me, 'Lord, Lord,' will enter the kingdom of heaven, but the one who does the will of my Father who is in heaven. On that day many will say to me, 'Lord, Lord, did we not prophesy in your name, and cast out demons in your name, and do many mighty works in your name?' And then will I declare to them, 'I never knew you; depart from me, you workers of lawlessness.'

Judas was a false apostle, but he was an apostle nevertheless. We cannot neglect the pertinence of understanding that Judas was an apostle. His unique character proved his heart to not be towards Jesus. We must be alert for those who move in the apostolic yet have a heart that will not hold up in the face of trials and temptations for Jesus.

Eight

Eight other apostles were named by Jesus. Although much is known about these men by oral tradition and writings such as those compiled by historians like Eusebius, the Bible makes very little known of their ministry. We know much less of the ministry of a majority of the original apostles than some of those later added.

-Andrew

What about Andrew, Simon Peter's brother? We know nothing of his ministry from the Bible after the baptism of the Holy Spirit.

-James

What about James, the other son of Zebedee? He was killed violently with the sword by Herod the King as recorded in Acts chapter twelve. He became the first apostle who was martyred.

-Philip

What about Philip? Many are unaware that there was even Philip the apostle. Most of us only know of Philip the evangelist, but these are not the same person. Philip the apostle is not recorded in Scripture following the baptism of the Holy Spirit.

-Bartholomew

What about Bartholomew/Nathanael? Too, we know nothing of his ministry from the Bible after the baptism of the Holy Spirit.

-Thomas

What about Thomas? What happened after Jesus removed his doubt? Once again, we know he was there during the baptism of the Holy Spirit, but the Bible records nothing of his ministry afterwards.

-James

What about the other James, the son of Alphaeus? Yet another biblically unidentified apostle. James only appears during the lists of the apostles.

-Judas

What about Judas/Thaddaeus? He is traditionally ascribed to be known as Jude who wrote the epistle of Jude. We at least have some reference to know that Jude did ministry after being called to be an apostle through his writings.

-Simon

What about Simon the Zealot? This Simon was found at the baptism of the Holy Spirit, but no more is given to readers from the Bible.

The original apostles ministries were so diverse. Many of them felt great significance to record their ministering for future generations to live by these testimonies. A majority, though, felt no need to write at all. They lived and died as apostles, but we have no knowing biblically of what their ministries entailed.

Other Apostles

A few others are attributed as apostles in the New Testament besides Jesus, the twelve, and Paul. In Acts chapter one, we see that the eleven remaining apostles cast lots for the Holy Spirit to guide them in the replacement of the apostleship of Judas. Matthias was selected over Justus.

Many within the ministry of Paul are also identified as apostles. Barnabas, the companion of Paul, also earns the title of apostle in the Bible as we see in Acts 14:14. In 1 Corinthians 4:9, contextually Paul identifies Apollos as an apostle. Silas and Timothy are both identified by Paul as apostles in his first letter to the Thessalonians (1:1 and 2:6).

Andronicus and Junias are the only apostolic couple mentioned in Scripture. As later scholars have abandoned this idea due to their diminishing of the apostolic and at times even misogyny, we cannot deny them being known among, that is as one, of the apostles.

Romans 16:7 (NASB) - Greet Andronicus and Junias, my kinsmen and my fellow prisoners, who are outstanding among the apostles, who also were in Christ before me

To what conclusion can we then come to about the apostolic? Was Paul out of line by naming others as apostles? No. The eleven replaced Judas not because there could only be twelve, but because the apostolic cannot be allowed to die within the church. Apostolic expansion should be both welcomed and expected by the church. We see that not all apostles have the same look. Not all apostles have the same sound. But all apostles have the same acts, which makes apostolic strategy the most powerful tool given by Christ for spiritual warfare.

Chapter 6:
Acknowledging the Devil's Children

As a child growing up, I was really good at following the rules. I was a 'good kid'. I did what I was told. I always completed my homework. I wasn't a troublemaker. I did good in school. I did all that I needed to do to be considered as good in the sight of people. I was even baptized at the age of 8 years old because that's what I was told I needed to do to get to spend eternity with God (but that didn't do much for my eternal state).

From that point in my life, I continued to walk and do what I was told needed to be done in order to be considered "good." I established my identity as one that was works based. If I do good, you will love me. If I do poorly, you won't. I believed that I must do good in order to be good.

After several more difficult life-changing events unfolded, I found myself questioning all that I thought and all that I believed. I began to search for meaning in my life. I sought for comfort through relationships and resources that would only temporarily sustain happiness in my life. I had a void. This legalistic mentality and lack of self-fulfillment and self-worth led me down a path of medically diagnosed depression. There were several times where I had planned out how I would end my life.

Then, I had a dear friend come to me. He told me that he had recently re-dedicated his life to Jesus. He told me that because God loves me so much, he could not stand to be separated from me, but my sins were causing just that. On February 27th, 2011 I gave my life to Christ and began a real relationship with a real God that really cares about me.

On that day, I was saved. I had been born again. My salvation was instant, but a process of sanctification had to begin. I had to re-evaluate my friendships, my behavior, my passions, my emotions, my desires, my thoughts, and even what spiritual doors I had open. Before we engage in any level of spiritual warfare, we must all do the same.

Relationships

1 Corinthians 15:33 - Do not be deceived: "Bad company ruins good morals."

Relationships are the most powerful influencers on earth. I've often been taught that our lives will look the most like the three people we spend the most time with. This affects every area of our lives. Along with that teaching came the sobering statistic that not only does lifestyle conform to those we spend the most time with, but that we likely will make within a $10,000 window of those we spend the most time with as well. Relationships can oftentimes mask what's going on internally.

I've considered why people are attracted to

one another. Why does it always seem that the abusive male finds the girl with an abusive past in the bar? What makes them always seem to find themselves around one another? Better yet, why do drug dealers always know who they can sell to in a crowd? Or, from the other end of the spectrum, why do believers find themselves chatting with one another at Walmart? The short answer: spirits click. There is constantly a realm of communication happening around us that we only tap into while praying in tongues. Spirits constantly are in communication. Angels are spiritual shepherds; while demons huddle around one another and draw communities together who will aid their agenda. Our relationships are always formed first in the spirit.

With that perspective, it gives us a whole new urgency to examine our relationships. Are we more surrounded with children of the King or the devil's kids?

Ephesians 2:1-2 - And you were dead in the trespasses and sins in which you once walked, following the course of this world, following the prince of the power of the air, the spirit that is now at work in the sons of disobedience—

There are two types of people in this world: followers of Jesus and followers of Satan. If we aren't for Christ, we are against him. The verse above can be understood in one of two ways: 1. Sons of disobedience are unbelievers. 2. Sons of disobedience are disobedient children of God. Although the first rendering is the correct understanding, we will still examine both thoughts for our growth in understanding relationships.

Relationships with unbelievers can be counterproductive to our Christianity. Let me clarify: we are called to have a relationship with unbelievers. We are to be in the world, yet not of the world. We cannot illustrate the love of Christ to the not yet saved if we do not have a connection with them. However, this connection can never become a primary influencer for our lives. Take for instance the teaching that a believer should not marry an unbeliever. This was revealed to the church so that we aren't lead astray into false beliefs. Those we spend the most time with will influence our worldview. If they aren't a Christian ("like-Christ"), then they can never help our lives to look like Christ.

Consider for a moment if this passage were referring to not unbelievers, but disobedient children of God. In other words, as the contemporary church claims it, the sons of disobedience are 'backslidden' believers. Believers who are not obedient to the call of God on their life have allowed just as much demonic influence over their actions as an unbeliever. We cannot let a rebellious spirit have any more say in our life than a Wiccan. If it seems absurd to let a practicing witch guide our lives closer to Christ, then we must conclude it is as absurd to allow a rebellious believer have that authority (*1 Samuel 15:23*). (And if any one thinks a witch can guide a believer closer to God, let them know they have believed the ultimate deception - no one can come to God except through Christ and his teaching alone.)

Relationships contribute to our lives. We ultimately are to examine if these influences affect us positively or negatively. We would all do better at who we allow into our lives if we understood that all relationships either produce equity or debt. In college my minor was Accounting. The accounting equation is: Assets = Liabilities + Equity. Ultimately, what most people want to know for their business or personal lives is what is the equity? At the end of the day am I profitable or losing money? This equation can be applied to our relationships as well. If a relationship doesn't bring more in (assets) than it pulls out from us (liabilities) than that relationship has negative equity, i.e. debt. Almost no relationship is neutral (pours in as much as it takes from). Not all debt relationships are unwarranted. For instance, my 20 month old daughter requires much more out of our relationship than she contributes from it. However, if we don't have more positive going in than we have being withdrawn, we begin to feel spiritually dry and can even enter into depression. As much as we have flowing out, we must also have being poured in by Holy Spirit and godly influencers. Those innermost relationships are either an asset to us or an overwhelming liability in our spiritual warfare.

Flesh

When it comes to living a Spirit-led life, living according to our flesh is the polar opposite end of the spectrum. Our spirit focuses on the eternal kingdom of God and our everlasting hope; the flesh is focused on maintaining enough for the temporal body we've been given to survive even a little longer.

Living by the flesh is a very self-centered lifestyle where the only focus is prolonging and advancement of myself. The Darwinian theory of evolution is a great example of living for the flesh: only the fit survive. This theory suggests that our sole purpose is to by any means live another day on the earth. Jesus commands us to bear our cross (*Luke 14:27*) and as Paul eloquently writes to die daily to our flesh (*1 Corinthians 15:31*).

Galatians 5:19-21 - Now the works of the flesh are evident: sexual immorality, impurity, sensuality, idolatry, sorcery, enmity, strife, jealousy, fits of anger, rivalries, dissensions, divisions, envy, drunkenness, orgies, and things like these. I warn you, as I warned you before, that those who do such things will not inherit the kingdom of God.

While sin may not stop a believer from inheriting salvation, living according to our flesh produces works which does limit our effectiveness for releasing the kingdom of God here on earth. If we are producing works of the flesh, we cannot at the same time produce works of the Spirit. The flesh stops the flow of the Spirit of God in our lives. Either we produce the gifts of the Spirit and his fruit or we are working according to the flesh.

Galatians 5:22-23 - But the fruit of the Spirit is love, joy, peace, patience, kindness, goodness, faithfulness, gentleness, self-control; against such things there is no law.

As we function according to the flesh, we are operating at the lowest level of thinking.

John 6:35 - Jesus said to them, "I am the bread of life; whoever comes to me shall not hunger, and whoever believes in me shall never thirst.

Jesus promises us that by following him, we can trust that our most basic needs for survival will be met. If we cannot trust God to provide for our basics here on earth, how could we trust him for an everlasting salvation relationship? The truth is if we are trapped according to the works of our flesh, the demonic will always have reign over our lives. We are living by the world, not our position in Christ.

Soul

Mark 8:36 - For what does it profit a man to gain the whole world and forfeit his soul?

The word translated as soul in Scripture is the Greek word that can be transliterated as psyche. It is the root word for our English word psychological. Our soul is what is actively engaged while reading this book. It is the part of our being we are most aware of, our conscious self. Soul is comprised of mind, will, and emotions. Within the soul, our mind should come first, followed by will, then emotions. Our soul is healthiest when our decisions come from that order. We should be able to make a decision in our mind whether we want to or feel like it. Paul encourages us that this order to our thought processes can be aligned by having the mind of Christ.

-Emotions

God created us as a triune being: spirit, soul, flesh. His creation, as we read in Genesis 1-2, was perfect. God created us in this triune manner to help us experience who he is and the love he has for us. God gave us our emotions as a type of sensor for what is going on within us and in our environment.

Matthew 9:36 - When he saw the crowds, he had compassion for them, because they were harassed and helpless, like sheep without a shepherd.

Emotions are meant to motivate us to minister. God is even made to be known as equal to love, not just the emotion side of it, but love in its pure form (*1 John 4:1*). Jesus, too, was a person who expressed his emotions healthily. We see this in the shortest verse in the Bible (*John 11:35*).

Emotions, though, should always be like a thermometer, not a thermostat. Emotions should help us to understand what is going on in our lives, not determine what will take place. When emotions dictate our actions, we are living in an unhealthy state. Emotions can be deceptive.

Emotional instability coupled with unresolved hurt (which is a habitat for unhealthy emotions to fester) will cripple us from fulfilling our God given purpose while on earth. Just as a wound in the flesh produces physical scar tissue, emotions act in a similar manner. When our flesh is cut deep, on the outside we may see a scar. On the inside the healthy flesh has been replaced with scar tissue. This tissue is interwoven and knotted up. It's not nearly as healthy or pretty, but is a defense mechanism by our body to protect our wounds. When we experience a wound that hurts our feelings, our natural way of handling this is to distance ourselves from those who have caused a wound. Unfortunately, we often times will lash out from this place of emotional hurt as well until we have resolved our feelings.

Revelation 21:4 - He will wipe away every tear from their eyes, and death shall be no more, neither shall there be mourning, nor crying, nor pain anymore, for the former things have passed away."

Emotions are a sensation for the earth which must be mastered.

<u>-Will</u>

Our will is our desire. Whatever we want to do or do not want to do determines what we ultimately will do. Whenever our desires do not align with the will of God, we begin to chase after passions of the flesh as opposed to the heart of God.

Our innermost desire is often expressed through our attitude. When it comes to emotional healing and experiencing the fullness of this world through our emotions, it is all contingent upon attitude. Without the correct attitude, emotions will overrule us. Attitude, the position of your heart, makes all the difference between sin and justified.

Ephesians 4:26-27 - Be angry and do not sin; do not let the sun go down on your anger, and give no opportunity to the devil.

We can have emotions and express those emotions without sinning, but the difference is our attitude. Jesus flipped tables out of anger, yet never sinned. The position of our heart dictates the expression of our soul.

Some days, I don't feel like getting up early. Some days I feel like believing I'm fighting the old man, when Scripture clearly says he is dead. Some days I don't feel like being a good role model; I just want to unplug from reality or blend into the crowd. Some days I feel like believing a lie and letting those old ways of thinking come back in. But if I don't have the right attitude, those emotions will run all over me. I'll live my life based on how I feel in the moment as opposed to the eternal truth we all submit to.

So what is God's will?

1 Thessalonians 5:16-18 - Rejoice always, pray without ceasing, give thanks in all circumstances; for this is the will of God in Christ Jesus for you.

God has a specific will regarding every situation in our lives. We see in this verse, though, the general will of God for all believers. First, we are to rejoice always. To rejoice is to release joy. Joy is a fruit of God's Spirit living within you. If our joy isn't coming from the Lord, it simply isn't coming at all. Second, we must pray without ceasing. Prayer is a fancy term used by Christian to describe communication with God. Prayer is communicating with God, which takes both speaking and listening. I would be terrible at communicating with my wife if I did all the talking or if I never responded when she spoke. Third, we must give thanks in all circumstances. If we are thankful, the enemy will have no room to move in. The enemy can only creep in when we are not grateful. There is no room for the enemy to move where we are thankful. Giving thanks shuts the door to the enemy.

God's desire is fairly basic: to have a relationship with the world. Our desires betray us when we desire things over people or people over God.

-Mind

If the devil can get in our mind, we will do all his work for him. The mind is the battlefield we will spend the most time over. The goal for every believer is to have the mind of Christ.

1 Corinthians 2:16 - "For who has understood the mind of the Lord so as to instruct him?" But we have the mind of Christ.

In order to receive this level of thinking, we must become aware of our thought life.

We are taught that when we are saved we are a new person, but still have to deal with our old ways of thinking, those old thought patterns. In the natural, once a thought pattern is established it creates what is referred to as a neuron highway or neurological pathways in the brain. Picture an image of a brain. The bumps and grooves that we imagine when we hear or read the word brain are those neurological pathways. Once we encounter a situation, our brain creates connections to tell our bodies how we should respond based on personal history if we ever encounter that situation again. The more often we respond to a set of circumstances the same way, the deeper the grooves become and the more difficult it is to break that way of thinking. This is a large clue as to why addiction to sin is so difficult to break. Biblically, though, the concept of us being stuck with our old ways of thinking after salvation is untrue.

2 Corinthians 5:17 - Therefore, if anyone is in Christ, he is a new creation. The old has passed away; behold, the new has come.

We are a new creation and have received the mind of Christ. After salvation, the Bible is no longer a book by which we contend to live towards. Jesus was the fulfillment of the Law and Prophets and established the new covenant. He gifted us this same position through salvation. In short, that means that upon salvation Scripture is no longer a standard to contend towards, but the standard in which we live from. The biblical promises and commandments are the starting point for the life of a believer, not the finish line. If any area of our lives does not match up to the standard of Scripture, we have a right as a believer to command that area to come to fruition, which includes our thought life.

As I previously detailed, I have been taught to stop repenting of thoughts that aren't mine. As referenced in the orange tree illustration, I know that if a thought is in my mind that is unbiblical then it did not originate inside of me. If I dwell on a thought, it deserves my repentance. If I spend all my time in fantasy, I will never live out the reality of the kingdom of God. However, if the thought isn't mine and I am healthily aligned where my mind is leading my will which leads my emotions and I am not making decisions solely upon the survival of my flesh, then I shift my attention to the spirit realm to engage in battle.

Spirit

After we come to a right positioning and alignment within our soul and flesh, we can direct our attention to the spiritual realm. If my soul and flesh are healthy, yet I still am not walking in the life that Christ gifted to me, then there must be spiritual influences at work.

Spiritual matters have highest level of influence over our life. Since the spirit is a higher influencer over us than our mind, many are unaware of the impact on their life. This is why it is so important for us to surround ourselves with other believers full of the Spirit of God who have been given his gifts, particularly discernment. The gifts of the Spirit reveal to us these unseen influencers in our life, especially when we are oppressed.

Jesus taught that if we aren't filled with his Spirit that the repercussion is being filled with demonic spirits. Typically this is defined as possession. However, there is also a point of what we call oppression. This can happen to believers and unbelievers alike. Oppression is not being owned or filled by demonic spirits but being taunted by them in the spiritual realm.

Some believe that demons are a thing of the past, or maybe even something of the Old Testament. Paul said this:

Acts 13:40-41 - Beware, therefore, lest what is said in the Prophets should come about: "'Look, you scoffers, be astounded and perish; for I am doing a work in your days, a work that you will not believe, even if one tells it to you.'"

Paul, here, quotes a verse from the book of Habakkuk stating that the Chaldeans will be raised up against the Jews. Many Jews in Paul's day would have made fun of Paul saying there are no more Chaldeans. In the natural, there were not. This people group had perished long before Paul. Paul, though. was speaking with an analogy to compare this cultural group to demons. He was saying you may say there are no more Chaldeans, but the spirit behind their lifestyle, which is demonic, is still present today.

People in modern times still live with that flawed mindset that demons are a thing of the past. It simply isn't true. The spiritual realm is more real than even what we can see with the physical eye. God existed in the spiritual realm before he ever spoke and created angels and humans. Spiritual warfare is constantly going on around us and the two sides are in opposition over our everlasting hope.

Chapter 7:
Strategies at War

During the coursework for the completion of Arkansas' Enhanced Concealed Carry Handgun License, I was challenged by my instructor concerning my tactical strategies. He began to challenge our thinking and preparedness regarding diverse scenarios that would require action for us to potentially use deadly force. I quickly realized that if I'm going to be prepared to use a weapon, I have to be prepared for the scenarios in which that weapon may be used. I cannot think from my perspective. I have to know the ways of the enemy.

He used an illustration to expound upon his thought. He said if a fire happens in the right front corner of the room and there is a large potted plant in the left front corner, a tarp in the right rear corner, and a bucket of water in the left rear corner of the room; which would we grab to stop the fire? Our unanimous response was to go get the water. That is logical thinking. Tactical thinking makes the most of what is near us during a time of crisis before seeking out a more long term solution. Tactical thinkers grab the plant and create a barrier to the fire out of the dirt. They then grab the tarp, as it is the next closest item, knowing fire cannot exist without oxygen. Finally, they retrieve the bucket of water to put out any remaining fire and cut down the smoke. The instructor used this scenario to challenge us on three thoughts we had concerning basic concealed carry.

First, he asked us how many rounds our magazines hold. If anyone in the class carried a revolver, they were limited to five or six rounds at the most. Those with sub-compact pistols may luck out with an extra round or two. Regular compact pistol can hold approximately a dozen rounds, while full size pistols can hold sixteen or more rounds. Logical thinking tells us that we should gravitate towards what is most concealable as we likely will never encounter a situation requiring deadly force. The instructor shared with us that the average shooter will hit their target around seventy percent of the time and that under stress our accuracy drops by half. Let's take the average carry of eight for the illustration (and that's considering with one in the chamber). A seventy percent accuracy with this handgun leaves me at my best situation with 5.6 shots on target. In a high stress situation, I would place a potential 2.8 shots on target. Real world math tells me that two out of my eight shots would make it to the target, only three if I am lucky. The instructor informed us that the average number of shots hit to stop an aggressor is three. This leaves the average every day carry pondering if it is even worth the carry.

This of course lead to the second topic of challenge: how many magazines do we carry? If we are going to carry low round firearms for concealability, we must consider carrying spare magazines. The tactical logic behind this is that most occurences in which firearms are involved report more than one individual present. If all of our rounds have been used to stop aggressor number one, what happens if they have an accomplice?

Finally, he asked us what types of bullets we carry in our magazines. He pulled the magazines out of his every day carry and unstacked them. We saw that he had three or four different types of rounds. First, there were frangibles. Then, there were various types of hollow points. Lastly, there were full metal jacketed rounds. He told us that as an instructor he is very practiced with his firearm. I would imagine his accuracy to be in the upper ninety percentile. The tactical thought is I want my first three rounds to not penetrate beyond target, as most conflicts are within just a few feet. Second, if these rounds don't stop them, perhaps I need more penetration. If I've used more rounds than the average person even carries and the aggressor is still posing a deadly threat, why? Have they moved somewhere with physical barriers to protect them. If so, solid rounds may be the only thing with enough penetration to stop that threat.

If we are going to be involved in spiritual warfare, please don't be the average Christian. We should not arm ourselves with just enough knowledge to leave us in the sights of the enemy without any more ammunition. We have to have tactic to our warfare. We must modify our own way of thinking, but we also have to be aware of how the enemy crafts his strategies. People who use weapons to create fear and steal the lives of others are bullies. They never consider what it is like for someone to stand against them and use that same deadly force to stop them.

James 4:7 - Submit yourselves therefore to God. Resist the devil, and he will flee from you.

<u>Demonic Strategy</u>

The entire demonic army is comprised of spiritual bullies as well. Every angelic being which is now classified as a demon once graced the walkways of heaven. As we read in Revelation chapter twelve, one third of the angels joined Satan in his rebellion against God and were cast out of heaven alongside him. These fallen angels now roam the earth alongside Satan seeking whom they can ensnare. Their attempt is to prevent all humanity from having an everlasting relationship with God which was abandoned by them. As they know what it was like to have a relationship with God and then lose it, they don't even want humans to experience for a moment the purity of being in God's presence.

Job 1:7 - The LORD said to Satan, "From where have you come?" Satan answered the LORD and said, "From going to and fro on the earth, and from walking up and down on it."

As previously mentioned, demons work in a spiritual hierarchy. Although their schemes are rooted in rebellion and deception, they still manage to have some level of respect for the work of one another. Individually, they desire to gain as much authority over the human race as possible to find some sense of pride and fulfillment by causing humans to experience the woes of hell which was created by God originally to house only fallen angels. Collectively, they coordinate their skills at provoking and alluring humans away from the goodness of God in hopes of maximizing their effects on the human race.

Demons coordinate through the leadership infrastructure of the demonic fourfold. We must keep in mind that Satan is the cornerstone of all that demons attempt to build on this earth. Satan, as with all demons for that matter, is a deceiver. There is nothing within a demonic angel which has the capability of creating something new. Every teaching and act of worship instilled by demonic forces is merely a mockery and manipulation of the true acts of worship towards God.

Other demons battle for their place in the demonic fourfold to achieve some rank of influence over their peers and the human race. The goal of this demonic fourfold is the same goal that God instilled to the fivefold ministry: to create a foundation in which the kingdom is built and expanded. Demons are attempting to build a false foundation by which they can lure people into the kingdom of Satan. When they successfully establish a foundation within the heart of a person or geographic area on this earth, we call that a stronghold.

Proverbs 10:29 - The way of the LORD is a stronghold to the blameless, but destruction to evildoers.

A stronghold in biblical times was a fortified city. When a city began to have enough resources and people in which they wanted to maintain community and protection from the outside world, they began to build walls around the city. These walls served two purposes. First, walls would protect what was inside from attacks and influence from the outside. Second, walls would foster what was inside to grow stronger and more influential. When a city was truly fortified and both of these purposes were taking place, the city was considered to be a stronghold.

Strongholds, spiritually, act in a similar manner. Whenever the ways of God are someone's stronghold, the beliefs about God are treasured and protected within the heart of that person. The heart of God becomes the heart of man. Additionally, God protects the believer from demonic infiltration. The Scripture tells us that we are sealed by his Holy Spirit until the day of salvation.

Contrarily, demonic strongholds are crafted in deception to cause the opposite to happen. When a person's life has given way to a demonic stronghold, demons protect evildoers and invoke destruction to the blameless. When this happens regionally, the demonic entity of influence attempts to fortify the city from the outside world. Demons want to prevent the love of God from penetrating their oppression. They ensure this takes place by incubating under their authority sin patterns growing stronger and more influential.

The expansion of the kingdom of Satan and the decline of the kingdom of God on earth is the number one priority of every single demon. Strongholds are the greatest tool the enemy has in expanding his influence within the earth. Once the walls of the stronghold are broken, regardless of if this occurs regionally or personally, we must attack the foundation. Once the foundation of demonic structure has been demolished, God's truth can be laid as the foundation. Christ can be the cornerstone and the kingdom of God can be built upon the foundation of the apostles and prophets.

While strongholds are the greatest ploy of the enemy, it is by no means his only tactic. The enemy loves to get in our face and isolate us from the body of Christ. We love to sing songs in regards to Jesus leaving the ninety-nine over the one sheep. However, we must understand that as the Good Shepherd, this verse was included because Jesus understands that the isolated believer is under far greater risk of being attacked than those who are gathered in unity. Isolation is the devil's favorite tactic against a believer.

John 10:10 - The thief comes only to steal and kill and destroy. I came that they may have life and have it abundantly.

While isolated, the enemy can pledge an onslaught of attacks upon us. He can coordinate demonic attacks to destroy us while we are isolated. The enemy desires to steal every physical blessing; kill our soul by vexing it to death; and destroy us spiritually through oppression and idolatry. Individually, he wants to flip our lives on their heads. He would love to see our mind in submission to desires and emotions which are gratifying the flesh, all under his demonic control.

If the devil cannot convince us to abandon the gathering, he will attempt to cause disunity among believers. If he cannot have control over our lives, he desires for believers to be in contention and prohibiting one another's good works. The devil loathes over disunity among the Church. He will do anything he can to demolish the strongholds of God and erode the foundation of God's kingdom here on earth. Consider for a moment all that the enemy has done to the physical temple of Solomon throughout history.

Psalm 11:3 - if the foundations are destroyed, what can the righteous do?"

Finally, demonic forces will coordinate together to attack those around us when he cannot touch our lives. There was a moment in my life when Natalie and I were doing great. We had even just birthed our first daughter. Life for us in that moment was going well. However, everyone around us was being attacked. Although I cannot recall all the attacks surrounding us, I will never forget the final ploy which dislodged our position. Our landlord passed away causing his newly widowed wife to have to move back into the home we were renting and forcing us into homelessness with our two month old daughter. If those surrounding our lives are under attack, we cannot dismiss this as an attack against us. The enemy will indirectly attack our lives when he cannot directly get to us. Indirect attacks are well calculated and can be against those close to us physically, spiritually, or even close to our hearts. If those around us are being attacked, we must be aware as the enemy may be indirectly attacking us. Indirect attacks hope to force us off of our path as the surroundings are disturbed.

Apostolic Strategy

Apostolic culture is not one of tolerance; it's one of love. My greatest fear is that future generations would view the love I have for humanity as a tolerance towards their sins. As previously detailed, the apostolic is very fatherly which is always accompanied by grace towards mistakes and an atmosphere of creative advancement. The apostles realize that the church cannot be all God intended without forward movement. The apostolic is a forerunner anointing. However, mercy cannot be corrupted as tolerance.

Revelation 2:20 - But I have this against you, that you tolerate that woman Jezebel, who calls herself a prophetess and is teaching and seducing my servants to practice sexual immorality and to eat food sacrificed to idols.

Not everyone on our leadership team agrees about tertiary issues. We all have a very concise view on dogmatic issues, but there are people who come to our church who disagree about doctrinal issues. Our church has an atmosphere of love. If there is disagreement about biblical viewpoints that should not separate us, we do not let it separate us; sin does not break our fellowship either regardless of who that individual is.

My desire for our leadership team is to remember this position is not because I tolerate false beliefs. I love them and know what is the core. We must create a firm foundation that will not allow future generations to erode and tolerate false teachings. Sadly, I see this happening across the United States in established churches, especially towards homosexuality.

Several homosexuals have come to LifeBridge throughout our time in Jonesboro. A few of them were very connected to our church. We loved them while they were with us and will continue to love those who come in the future. Contrarily, we asked them to not participate in public displays of affection, as we would any couple who got out of hand at church services. We also held a very firm stance on the fact they are welcome, but the Bible clearly states homosexuality and all sexual immorality is sin.

Toleration towards sin cripples the Church. This has gone on since God established a people. God warned the Israelites before they took the promised land to not take foreign wives because he knew their heart. When we allow those who are involved in sin to become key influencers in our lives, we will be led away from the promises of God. Ergo, our casualty rate will increase and effectiveness, especially awareness, in spiritual warfare greatly diminishes. Every apostolic strategy is built upon the love of Christ towards his people.

Apostolic Defense

Apostles and apostolic ministries do not have to defend themselves. My Pastor has often reiterated to me to always apologize if someone has taken offense, even if I believe I am not guilty of their accusations. While this is entirely true, it doesn't capture the fullness of all I mean by the previous statement. Apostolic ministries do not have to strive to defend themselves spiritually. Daily, we are called to consciously put on the armor of God. However, our defenses are far stronger than those few pieces of armor.

Psalm 5:12 - For you bless the righteous, O LORD; you cover him with favor as with a shield.

The favor of God is the protection by which we live our lives. We should not live in constant fear of what the enemy could potentially do to our lives. God has gifted us with faith and this faith is our personal shield. Yet beyond that we are covered by the canopy of God's favor. His favor shields his children from demonic attacks.

Secondly, God himself conducts warfare on behalf of his children. It is quite comforting to consider that double Satan's army is God's angelic army. However, Habakkuk records that God himself even gets involved in defending his children from demonic spiritual attacks.

Habakkuk 3:14 - You pierced with his own arrows the heads of his warriors, who came like a whirlwind to scatter me, rejoicing as if to devour the poor in secret.

If that verse doesn't get us excited about the freedom we can experience even in the midst of spiritual warfare, nothing will. Habakkuk writes about God's involvement in spiritual warfare with such vivid imagery. I imagine the battle scene to look like this:

Satan sends forth his demonic army which clashes into the angelic army with such force. As this warfare is being waged above our heads over our soul, we haven't a clue the significance it truly will have in our lives. Our faith has run weary from the ongoing battle. At that time, a demon releases a flaming dart directed toward our heart from his own fiery bow. It somehow penetrates beyond the shields and looks as though it will soon make a fatal blow in our life. Suddenly, God appears standing slightly ahead of us and sticks his arm out catching the arrow in mid-flight. He flips the arrow around as a spear and stabs that same demon directly between the eyes.

Knowing that God defends me is all the defense I need in this life. Ignoring spiritual warfare for a moment, consider how freeing life would be if we trusted God to stab our enemies in the face with their own attacks against us. This is the heart behind my pastor's statement of encouragement. We need not try to defend ourselves but humbly apologize knowing what is being said is an attack that God shields us from and fights back towards.

We must remind ourselves that what is so violently attacked by the devil should reveal our greatest level of authority in the kingdom of God. For instance, if our prayer language is attacked, we have been graced to make a great impact by speaking in tongues.

Apostolic Offense

- Holy Boldness

There are a few different tactics that aid in apostolic offense strategies. First, is boldness.

Matthew 11:6 - And blessed is the one who is not offended by me."

Jesus was offensive in his preaching style. It takes an offensive church to save the world from an eternity in hell. In our culture, it appears to be popular to be offended. However, our churches should be offensive to the enemy. We can either be offended by that or join in on the offensive strategy; it's your choice. The difference between offense and offense is simply how it's pronounced; it's perspective.

Acts 4:31 - And when they had prayed, the place in which they were gathered together was shaken, and they were all filled with the Holy Spirit and continued to speak the word of God with boldness.

In this passage, Peter and John were just released from speaking before the council. These two must have been extremely nervous to face the same trials that Jesus did before his crucifixion. This passage tells us that the council knew that these men had been with Jesus because of their boldness even though they were uneducated, common men. However, after the trial, Peter and John asked for the other believers to pray for their boldness to be replenished. They, along with everyone in the room, were filled with the Holy Spirit again. They Holy Spirit is the forerunner in all spiritual matters, especially warfare.

We cannot separate the Holy Spirit from any spiritual matter. He is the core that gives us boldness. Without the infilling of the Holy Spirit, we are a hollow person incapable of standing firm against the schemes of the devils.

- Tongues

The tongue is the most powerful instrument God gave humanity. I believe the crux of humanity being formed in the image of God is the fact that we can speak! With God's speech, he created existence, and our tongue is granted the power of life and death.

Proverbs 18:21 - Death and life are in the power of the tongue, and those who love it will eat its fruits.

It is an instrument of fire. Our tongue will be on fire: either with the fire of hell or the fire of God. However, most of us speak in the wrong language, even if we speak in a tongue - because that's what most of us access. Even if we move in the gifts of the Holy Spirit, we just speak in a tongue because we don't know how to truly speak in tongues.

There are primarily 4 types or categories of tongues in Scripture. First, is the disambiguation of praying in the Spirit. Prayers lead by the prompting of the Holy Spirit, not ones we conjure up, are prayers in the Spirit. This means these prayers can be either in earthly or angelic language.

1 Corinthians 13:1 - If I speak in the tongues of men and of angels, but have not love, I am a noisy gong or a clanging cymbal.

Jesus prayed in the Spirit. Every prayer Jesus prayed on earth was not in his native tongue. Jesus naturally speaks a heavenly language and Aramaic would have been learned by him on the earth. Even while on earth, though, we see Jesus praying in the Spirit.

Luke 10:21 - In that same hour he rejoiced in the Holy Spirit and said, "I thank you, Father, Lord of heaven and earth, that you have hidden these things from the wise and understanding and revealed them to little children; yes, Father, for such was your gracious will.

A lot of the church has been deceived into thinking tongues exists in a natural language only, which is completely unbiblical. While praying in the Spirit may be a supernatural gifting to pray in an earth language that was previously unknown, praying in the Spirit is a general term that could be prayers in a natural language led by the Holy Spirit or any of the following tongues.

Second, speaking in tongues can be a private prayer language.

1 Corinthians 14:2 - For one who speaks in a tongue speaks not to men but to God; for no one understands him, but he utters mysteries in the Spirit.

Private prayer language is our one-on-one love language with God. Once couples are in a longstanding relationship, they begin to have a pet language that no one else understands. That is similar to our private prayer language; no one else understands but God and the spirit of the person praying.

Take for instance hallelujah. What does hallelujah mean? The reason an answer doesn't immediately come to mind is the same reason hallelujah is left untranslated in our language. Hallelujah was introduced in the writings of David and is part of his private praise to God. When we say hallelujah, our minds have no definition for this word, but it resonates with our spirit.

Therefore, our private prayer language may come with or without interpretation as its design is to build up our spirit not our minds.

1 Corinthians 14:14-15 - For if I pray in a tongue, my spirit prays but my mind is unfruitful. What am I to do? I will pray with my spirit, but I will pray with my mind also; I will sing praise with my spirit, but I will sing with my mind also.

Not all the time is it beneficial for our flesh to know what the Spirit is praying through us on our behalf. At times, God wants us to really pray into something but he cannot trust us to fully reveal to us what that is at certain chronological times. He is awaiting a kairos moment to share that with us. Our private prayer language grants us the benefit of full access to godly prayer: the Spirit of God amplifies our prayers to the heavenlies where they are heard by Jesus and he intercedes on our behalf as he sits at the right hand of the Father.

Third, the most controversial tongue is corporate prophecy. Translated tongues in a corporate setting is equal to prophecy.

1 Corinthians 14:5 - Now I want you all to speak in tongues, but even more to prophesy. The one who prophesies is greater than the one who speaks in tongues, unless someone interprets, so that the church may be built up.

Paul never discourages the church from giving a corporate tongue. He does say that without interpretation it is unfruitful and less beneficial. Conversely, Paul also says he prays in tongues more than all those seated in that local church and if there is no one to interpret then we should pray in our private prayer language in a non-distracting manner.

Fourth, the most beneficial to this book and the most overlooked tongue is warfare tongues.

Ephesians 6:16-18 - In all circumstances take up the shield of faith, with which you can extinguish all the flaming darts of the evil one; and take the helmet of salvation, and the sword of the Spirit, which is the word of God, praying at all times in the Spirit, with all prayer and supplication. To that end, keep alert with all perseverance, making supplication for all the saints,

A few years back, I learned that the sword included in the armor of God referenced a Roman sword. The swords carried by Roman guards were not the longsword we often imagine. These swords were more like daggers and were carried around for soldiers to tend to their wounds when the flaming darts of the enemy happened to get beyond their shields. It makes logical sense that the word of God is beneficial by the Spirit to bring about our healing. This left me asking some serious questions though.

If the sword was not meant as an attack weapon, did God give us an armor just to not feel as beat up as the devil hurls flaming darts our way? No. He wants you to attack the devil. Jesus launched an offensive church. The part of the armor of God most often left out: praying at all times in the Spirit. Speaking in tongues is our attack weapon from the armor of God. Some of us think we enjoy warfare, but we've been talking to the devil in a language that he does not even speak. We've been speaking to him all sweet like we're talking to our Daddy God when we need to put that demon in his place. If we want to really freak the devil out, we tell him to get out of our house in his language. There are tongues designated for warfare, war cries in the Spirit! These are our most precious weapon for destroying strongholds.

- Angels

Worship is warfare in the spirit. When we enter into worship, we create an atmosphere of heaven around us. Supernaturally, the spirit realm shifts when we enter into worship. We push back the presence of the enemy and create a stronghold for angels to come and engage with us in the spiritual shifts.

Matthew 4:11 - Then the devil left him, and behold, angels came and were ministering to him.

As Jesus relied on the presence of angels to minister to him after an onslaught of demonic attacks administered by the hand of Satan, so too we must learn to become more sensitive to the presence of angels. Angelic encounters were a regular part of life in biblical times. From Sodom and Gomorrah to the birth of Jesus, angels accompany the praise and worship of God and they are an integral aspect of spiritual warfare.

In Daniel chapter ten, an angel was coming to minister to Daniel and was hindered by a demonic principality which had gained authority over that region. The battle was so intense that it escalated into the upper echelon of angelic authority for both sides.

Daniel 10:13-14 - The prince of the kingdom of Persia withstood me twenty-one days, but Michael, one of the chief princes, came to help me, for I was left there with the kings of Persia, and came to make you understand what is to happen to your people in the latter days. For the vision is for days yet to come."

Even when the group prayed for Peter's release from prison early on in the book of Acts, they were more expectant to see his angel than Peter himself. That should stir up our faith knowing that each of us has an angel assigned to minister alongside us. We should also come to expect to interact with the angelic realm. We cannot be engaged in spiritual warfare against fallen angels and not expect godly angels to be present. Welcome them in your praise (they were created for the praise of God) and join with them in spiritual battles.

- Testimony

Scripture only equates one thing as powerful as the blood that Jesus sacrificed on the cross at Calvary. Although this sounds erroneous, it is true. Our individual testimonies will do as much damage to the works of Satan collectively as what Jesus did on the cross.

Revelation 12:11 - And they have conquered him by the blood of the Lamb and by the word of their testimony, for they loved not their lives even unto death.

The Greek word which we render as testimony is most correctly defined as to do it again. When we share our testimony, whether of salvation or any move of God in our life, we command a spiritual atmosphere for God to be able to do again in that moment what was previously done in our witness. I have seen people baptized in the Holy Spirit and others physically healed without anyone ever laying hands on these individuals; their spirit responded to the testimonies being shared around them.

-#inJesusname

Devils are removed by our testimony and the name of Jesus. What Jesus did on the cross has more impact than we will ever phathom on this planet. What was released in the blood of Jesus is the most potent love this world has ever known. Yet we make a mockery of it often times when we pray.

Praying in Jesus' name is much more than a hashtag at the end of our social media post; it's more than a signature at the end of the email we are sending to "Santa"-God in hopes we get our presents. We truly pray in the name of Jesus by praying with his character, under his authority, and as his representative. Bringing the letters of the name of Jesus without his presence is the most dangerous mistake we can make in spiritual warfare.

Acts 19:13-16 - Then some of the itinerant Jewish exorcists undertook to invoke the name of the Lord Jesus over those who had evil spirits, saying, "I adjure you by the Jesus whom Paul proclaims." Seven sons of a Jewish high priest named Sceva were doing this. But the evil spirit answered them, "Jesus I know, and Paul I recognize, but who are you?" And the man in whom was the evil spirit leaped on them, mastered all of them and overpowered them, so that they fled out of that house naked and wounded.

Apostolic offense strategies include a well rounded plan to boldly deploy angels, worship God in his Spirit, proclaim the testimonies, and bring about the presence of Jesus on this earth again. They come from individuals who rightly align their spirit over the soul over the flesh and walk in the protection of God. These individuals are granted spiritual authority by their favor with both God and man; they empower other believers to fulfill the call of God in their life. Unity of believers is the force behind apostolic strategy.

Over the final few chapters, I share apostolic strategy concerning three of the greatest threats to the church. I could have written a prayer book. However, I would rather teach future generations how to pray than merely provide us with the words to say.

Chapter 8:
Warfare - Religion

The hardest spiritual attacks on my life have come from the spirit of religion. After feeling a void in my life at the age of eight years old, I was instructed that I needed to be baptized with no true connection with Jesus being mentioned. I remember even then after the service was over and everyone was congratulating me that I was confused about the significance of baptism. At the age of twenty-one, I began a real relationship with a real God that really cares about my life. That reality must mean that for nearly thirteen years I walked on this earth believing that I was saved, yet if I would have passed I would have spent eternity separated from God in hell.

My salvation freed me from the personal enslavement to religion, but I still battled the effects of the spirit of religion for several years following my salvation. Even surrendering to ministry did not stop the warfare of religion; it actually perpetuated it. Upon being accepted into seminary, I was forced to sign a covenant to go to school there. This covenant included one of the worst ploys of religion in our times. In order to go to pastoral school, I had to agree to not pray in tongues during my time at seminary. Ignorance of the ramifications of this as a new believer caused me to sign a covenant that would take me years to break and fully repent.

Religion

Religion is the most dangerous demon we battle as believers. I view only one other demon as significant as religion, witchcraft - which we examine in the following chapter. Religion and witchcraft are the demonic twins at the height of demonic influence. All other demonic spirits work to aid their influence. While witchcraft attempts to fool unbelievers that there is more power outside the church than from God, religion attempts to fool believers that God is powerless.

Religion is often titled as legalism in our culture. Religion is birthed in the attempt to practice following the laws of God without first understanding his heart; striving to meet the standard without having a relationship. Religion is often tied with a performance based identity.

Believers in God desire to have a relationship with him and work towards the laws God has given us for success in that relationship. While this sounds appealing at first glance, we cannot work our way into salvation. Salvation is gifted to us through a relationship first with Christ.

James 2:19 - You believe that God is one; you do well. Even the demons believe—and shudder!

Belief in God is the start of a relationship with him, but it is not all we need. Belief alone is not salvation. We have to trust in the redemptive work of Jesus, repent of sin, and allow God to also be our Lord. Once we receive salvation, the laws then become the standard in which we live our life from.

The issue with religion is that it slowly creeps into well-meaning hearts. We must first realize that we can have good intentions and still be dead wrong. Religion, while striving to meet the standard, places additional barriers to our relationship with God.

There is a vicious cycle: I want to have a relationship with God; I see his standard, yet I cannot reach his standard. I try to reach his standard and am disappointed when that standard is not met. This causes shame in my life. The only way I can conceive of how to reach this standard is via religion. I create my own set of rules and regulations which I believe will empower me to fulfill the standards of God. However, now I do not meet my own standards. This causes further disappointment and shame. At this point, I would believe myself to be unworthy to enter the presence of God for forgiveness as I cannot even meet my own 'helps' let alone God's laws. This is where demonic empowerment comes in. The more I fall short in my own standards the more laws I put in place and the farther I am propelled away from God. I therefore have become my own god and have thereby concluded that I am not worthy of forgiveness.

Even the demons believe. Even the demons know the Scriptures. But they have no relationship with God. People can be the exact same.

Matthew 3:7 - But when he saw many of the Pharisees and Sadducees coming to his baptism, he said to them, "You brood of vipers! Who warned you to flee from the wrath to come?

The very people who Jesus was sent to save were the ones who were responsible for his crucifixion. The Pharisees, Sadducees, and priests in Jesus' time on earth were believers in God, yet they had their own rules and ideals of what that relationship would look like. Their ideologies were so skewed that when God stood before them and looked them in the eyes, they did not recognize him. They were deceived by the lies of religion.

Lies

There are three lies that are promoted by demons of religion in order to get believers to think that God is powerless within the lives of his people. The first lie is the old adage of "well I'm just a lowly sinner saved by grace." While the words of this statement appear to be true, recall that demons can say the right words yet move in the wrong spirit. Upon salvation, we are adopted into the family of God (Galatians 4:5). The old man is dead (Romans 6:4) and a new being lives (2 Corinthians 5:17). When we confess the words of sinner over our lives, we have identity dysphoria and are empowering sin strongholds. In other words, if I confess to be a sinner, I must still be sinning or my identity is not validated. Religion works in this way to keep us adding rules to not meet God's standards but also by adding rules to ensure we always accept even a little sin on this side of the cross.

The second lie that the spirit of religion works through is the thought that if we know Scripture then we know God. I know a lot about our President. I've known about the works of President Trump since his days on the reality television show The Apprentice. During college, I studied some of the different businesses and tactics used by President Trump in his businesses. However, there is one fact that I know about President Trump that many do not know about even God: as much as I know about President Trump, he has not the slightest clue who I am. We can know so much about God and he have not a clue who we are. We can study his moves and know his Word, yet still not have a relationship with him. Immediately following Jesus' forty day fast prior to the start of his ministry, Jesus was tempted by the demonic world three times. In each of these attacks by Satan, the tempter challenged the identity of Jesus. However, in one attempt the devil even quoted Scripture (Matthew 4:6). Knowing Scripture, even moving in the power of the spiritual realm, does not equate to a relationship with Jesus (Matthew 7:21-23).

The third lie most often used by religious spirits is a direct attack against God himself. While no believer would say that God is powerless, religion has convinced many that his power has been compromised. Religion wants believers to feel hopeless even when they have the Living Hope of Christ Jesus. Religion works through legalism and mockery to get believers to follow moves of history with greater weight than the moves of God. What I am suggesting is that many have laid down the promises of God on the altar of religion out of good intention. Jesus says that he is leaving the earth for the greater good of mankind that his Promise may dwell among all humanity (John 14:26). This promise was and still is Holy Spirit. Religion convinces believers that the gifts were only meant for the elect and that God does not need to move in the same way in his church in modern times since we are established and have his written word. The Pharisees also led their churches through the written word of God, but they killed the greatest move of God in history. If Satan convinces the church that the gifts of God (i.e. Holy Spirit's gifts) are unnecessary for the church, he has successfully silenced God in his own house. If demons convince us that Holy Spirit's manifestations are not needed in the church, they have successfully removed God from the church. Thinking that removing Holy Spirit's presence from services increases the opportunity for the lost to find Jesus is a lie.

John 14:26 - But the Helper, the Holy Spirit, whom the Father will send in my name, he will teach you all things and bring to your remembrance all that I have said to you.

How can Holy Spirit teach us if we force his silence within the church? That's the goal of religion. Believing that lie belittles God within our church.

Truth

We've probably all heard the rumors by now that demons are legalistic. This is true, at least for some demons - those that are legalistic. Not every demon is legalistic in nature. For instance, rebellious demons are by nature rebellious. However, religious spirits are by nature legalistic. They look for us to improperly use scripture as an open entryway into our lives. I assert that religion is the most dangerous because it has been the favored scheme of Satan himself throughout history.

Genesis 3:1 - Now the serpent was more crafty than any other beast of the field that the LORD God had made. He said to the woman, "Did God actually say, 'You shall not eat of any tree in the garden'?"

These demons have to be spoken to directly and correctly or they will maintain legal access to our lives.

An important tactic in dealing with religious spirits is to understand that their legalistic ways bind them to chronological time. Satan opposed Jesus through religious ploys throughout his time on earth. Due to the nature of his tactics, he was not allowed to bring harm to Jesus until Jesus gave him the time. We see this theme throughout the gospel of John.

John 2:4 - And Jesus said to her, "Woman, what does this have to do with me? My hour has not yet come."
John 7:30 - So they were seeking to arrest him, but no one laid a hand on him, because his hour had not yet come.
John 16:32 - Behold, the hour is coming, indeed it has come, when you will be scattered, each to his

own home, and will leave me alone. Yet I am not
alone, for the Father is with me.
John 17:1 - When Jesus had spoken these words,
he lifted up his eyes to heaven, and said, "Father,
the hour has come; glorify your Son that the Son
may glorify you,

We must understand that the spiritual battle we
face, especially those with demons of religion, are
chronological events. As we transition our lives into
kairos moments ordained by God, we will indeed be
able to bind legalistic attacks to an hour that has
passed and walk beyond them.

Commissioning Decree

I'm not one to get loud very often in
preaching nor spiritual warfare. My victories come
from my position as much as they come from my
petition. However, decreeing the truth over our
lives, regardless of the volume, sets the
atmosphere for God to move. When we decree, we
commission the angels and position ourselves in
the flow of Holy Spirit.

To commission is to co-mission. It is to align
the mission of our lives with the mission of God. We
are called to co-labor with Christ, yet our labor is in
vain if we are not laboring for the same mission as
God. To commission someone is to release them to
fulfill the same mission. Jesus sent out his disciples
with the Great Commission, our mission and
commissioning must align with this original mission
of God to be effective. Commissioning the angels is
not commanding them but is merely revealing to
them the heart behind our strategy in which they

can then move alongside. Silence is the killer of the great moves; dialogue creates unity.

Here is a commission to aid in warfare against religion in our lives:

In the name of Jesus Christ I bind up every legalistic action and thought.

I release the angels to come alongside this word and push back the influence of religion over my life and region.

I bind every hindering spirit that would oppose these words.

I bind up religion and say that legalism has no hold over my life.

Jesus fulfilled the law and I am empowered by his love and Holy Spirit to fulfill his word.

I am not forced to love God and my actions no longer separate me from his presence.

The blood of Jesus covers my life and I will be free to fulfill the law because of my love for God.

I receive around my life discernment through the supernatural gifting of the Holy Spirit and other believers in which I trust.

God, I thank you for wisdom is found in sound council.

I pray favor over those who are my spiritual covering and who pour into my life.

I declare they will have godly insight and direction for me.

I receive breaker anointing from those who cover me.

God I believe the truth of your word.

I thank you that Paul was divinely inspired by Holy Spirit to author a letter to the church at

Rome and I know that the truths he revealed to them are still applicable to my life today.

I declare Romans 8:37-39 over my life today:

Romans 8:37-39 - No, in all these things we are more than conquerors through him who loved us. For I am sure that neither death nor life, nor angels nor rulers, nor things present nor things to come, nor powers, nor height nor depth, nor anything else in all creation, will be able to separate us from the love of God in Christ Jesus our Lord.

Testimony

As previously mentioned, sharing testimonies sets the atmosphere for God to do again in our lives what he previously has done. That fact is much of the power behind quoting Scripture. Also, sharing testimonies of our personal experiences with God or the experiences of others in which we are currently contending for does move the heart of God in a similar manner. I believe my testimony of becoming free from the religious spirit will move the atmosphere for God to release the same freedom from heaven into the midst of those who receive it.

It took me several years to break the hold of the religious demons off of my life. This was not due to a lack on God's part, nor was it due to some overwhelming power the enemy found over me. My bondage was due to my own ignorance.

Once I finally began to understand the spiritual matters of this life, I began to direct my attention to the real enemy. I became healthy in my flesh, my soul, and my own spirit, yet I still was being challenged in my relationship with God. I know that my choice could have been to experience God only in ways which made me comfortable, but I desired to experience God in the ways in which he desired for me to know him. Seeking God broke religion off of my life.

I know that sounds simple and that those who are under religion's influence have the heart to seek God as well, but truthfully they stop desiring God at points in which he makes them uncomfortable. I have believers very dear to my heart that confess they do not believe in speaking in tongues and that it is likely due to the fact that they haven't searched it out for themselves. Yet they still take no time to see if it is valid.

Once I sought God no matter how it made me feel, I realized that I had put a covenant with man higher than my covenant with God. I agreed to not allow God move in my life while I was at seminary because it made the denomination uncomfortable. The truth that set me free I also learned in seminary. During my time in seminary, the most powerful teaching I encountered was by far the simplest: 'If it is in the Bible preach it; if it is not then do not preach it.' In essence I learned that I cannot add to nor take away from Scripture in order to get my point across. I remember once that was said I had the ease in knowing I did not have to concern myself with preaching about tongues because Jesus never taught on the baptism of the Holy Spirit, until I realized that he did. Once I saw that this was something Jesus regularly taught on in his ministry, I could not take away from my preaching. I then was challenged that in order to preach it that I must understand it. The wrestling in my understanding of what this meant lead me to the convictions in which I live my life by even to this day.

Jesus taught on the baptism of the Holy Spirit. The Bible does not teach that this is to end nor does it teach an end to the apostolic ministry. Jesus gifts the church with five ministers to empower the church to fulfill its purpose on earth. We cannot add to nor take away from scripture; that is religion. Religion will not hold me back from getting to know God and experiencing as much of heaven on earth as I am called to steward.

Prayer

Prior to praying the suggested prayer below to break off attacks of religious demons, I encourage all to spend time praying in tongues. As we pray in tongues, we position ourselves in the spirit realm. We should empty of self and allow Holy Spirit to fill every fiber of our being. Align spirit over soul over flesh and envision the heavenly funnel being poured down. The angels stand behind us anticipating our war cries.

Father, I come to you in the name of Jesus. God I renounce every tie in my life to religion. I will not place my own regulations or man-made rules higher than your word. I believe that I am your child and I will receive my inheritance regardless of my feelings. Do not allow me to be deceived based on my desires to fulfill my pleasures. Protect me with your favor. Shield me and cover me with your grace. Father I move under your authority and I press in to know you more even when it makes me uncomfortable. Let me see and move in your heart and not to seek your hand.

Holy Spirit, I thank you for the ministering angels being sent forth right now in the spirit to accompany my words and see them come to full fruition. I repent of every soul tie I have made and every door that I have opened willingly or even unknowingly to the works of religion. Holy Spirit teach me to live from the promises you scribed in the Bible and not to strive in angst towards them.

Jesus I thank you for defeating religion time and time again during your time on earth. I pray that your life would be a model for me to live by: in perfect relationship with God regardless of the schemes of the devil. Thank you for laying down your life Jesus at the right time and putting an ultimate end to legalism in your Church. I pray that heaven would invade earth and your Church would be set free from false religion. Help me to be an ambassador of your presence here on earth starting within my local church. Jesus, I pray these things in your name. Amen.

Chapter 9:
Warfare - Witchcraft

My time in seminary was spent in one of our nation's most premier port cities, New Orleans. While New Orleans is not known by the world for its seminary, it is well-known for football, beignets, and Mardi Gras. New Orleans is a cultural powerhouse and is a ripe environment for evangelism.

I remember that my zeal quickly captured the admiration of my newest friends in seminary. We had arrived the week before school was to start in order to settle into our new life and city. I vividly recall sitting outside of the library before school started and everyone asking what we were going to do over the weekend. Most wanted to go downtown as I did, but I was the only one who wanted to evangelize the Wiccans.

Jackson Square sits in the heart of New Orleans. At the forefront of Jackson Square is the St. Louis Cathedral and at its feet the boardwalk. St. Louis Cathedral is one of the most historically rich churches in our nation and it has overlooked some of the most devastating times in our nation's history. In times passed, St. Louis Cathedral overlooked the auction house where slaves were sold upon immediately docking into our nation.

Currently, it overlooks Jackson Square where entertainers, artists, and Wiccans set up to dispense their goods.

We had just left Cafe du Monde when I directed our group towards the back of Jackson Square where St. Louis Cathedral resides. I could feel my blood pumping as I recalled the story of Jesus flipping tables as money-handlers exchanged goods at the temple doors and rehearsed my lines. I decided not to go to the far side of the Square as that's where the most intense divination occurred; some on that side of the garden even believed themselves to be brides of Satan. At the time, I was much more affluent in gospel presentation than I was in conversation. I spotted my target and my friends drew back; they decided it was best to not overwhelm him even though I knew they were timid.

I boldly approached a man dressed in all black. He was the stereotypical warlock with the imagery a cross between a wizard and magician. His gothic nature only drew me in towards him. I knew that he needed Jesus, but he was consumed with the demonic power. As I got closer I could see him shuffling through the Tarot cards along with other demonic toys. He greeted me with a smile and asked if he could share with me what he saw about my future. I assertively told him that I would give him a few minutes of my time as long as he would do the same. He comically retorted, "You must be one of those kids from that school." I was taken aback. He shared with me that he had heard it all before and that he was not interested in what I had to say. Honestly, I look back and thank God that he stopped that man from spewing curses over

137

my life when in my ignorance I did not have a clue how to break those off.

After that day, I have since been told by an individual that they wanted nothing to do with God if they could not see his power. They were immersed in the spiritual happenings of the demonic and had not experienced the same from God nor his Church. Some are simply allured by the authority of Satan and his manifestations. They do not have a clue that he is only a manipulator and deceiver. They have never encountered the true power of God and as the Church we've done a poor job at releasing it around them.

Description

Witchcraft is the demonic manifestation of the spirit realm. By nature, witchcraft is manipulative. No demonic entity has within itself the power to create something new. Everything experienced in the demonic realm is a twisting and perversion of godly ways. Manifestations of witchcraft are imposters to true manifestations of the Spirit of God. Even the practice of witchcraft was schemed as a mockery towards biblical worship.

Witchcraft, or as some translations say sorcery, is a direct translation from the Greek word which we transliterate as pharmakeia. As one can easily render, the Greek root word is the same root word in which we get our modern understanding of pharmaceuticals, medicine. An often times underlying stronghold of witchcraft is a chemical dependency and addiction. The chemical dependency is the fuel used for demons to manifest. When our bodies are not 'sober-minded,' we are weak and incapable of battling off thoughts which are not our own. Although modern medicine does amazing feats, we even have many in the medical field on the lay staff of our local church, we must begin to question the spiritual ramifications of when a body becomes dependent upon a drug.

While religion is a direct attack on God's supremacy, witchcraft annihilates the second commandment.

Exodus 20:4 - "You shall not make for yourself a carved image, or any likeness of anything that is in heaven above, or that is in the earth beneath, or that is in the water under the earth.

Even though the verse is just an excerpt from the second commandment, it provides us with enough truth to see how witchcraft targets those outside the church. Religion brings other gods into God's house. Witchcraft is riddled with idolatry. Religion serves an idle God; witchcraft serves idol gods.

Witchcraft, in many expressions, bears the face of polytheism. The worship of multiple gods is witchcraft. The belief in multiple routes to heaven, is witchcraft. Divination, addiction, and incantations are all various forms of witchcraft. Witchcraft moves in vain imaginations.

When we spend our lives in fantasy (not merely sexual, but any false reality), we have been engaged in the lies of witchcraft. Witchcraft attempts to cause us to believe that the reality that is experienced with God's Church and Kingdom is not enough to satisfy us. Witchcraft causes us to long for more. When the church does not provide what we desire, we leave. When our marriage does not provide what we desire, we step out. When life is not going the way we desire, we numb ourselves with alcohol and drugs. Witchcraft is the scheme of the devil to get us to live in a world that does not even exist.

Lie

The lies of witchcraft work hand-in-hand with the lies from religion. As with religion, we see three lies that demons of witchcraft loathe to promote. However, as religion works inside to outward, witchcraft begins outside the church and then slips inside. The greatest lie of witchcraft is that there are multiple spiritual authorities. Witchcraft dismisses the true sovereignty of God. Demons of witchcraft fool individuals into thinking they can access supernatural power and provision through means other than the one true God. Many of those who practice witchcraft believe in God; they assert that he is one of many though. Many of those who practice witchcraft believe in the afterlife; they just are not certain that heaven is any better than hell. Many of those who practice witchcraft believe in Jesus; they group him in as a good teacher or perhaps an oracle or prophet at best. Witchcraft's best deception is through confusion via choice paralysis.

The second lie we see witchcraft establish dominance through is fooling those who have been hurt or offended by the church. Spirits of witchcraft long for people to go to church and not experience change. They work hand in hand with religion to assure that what is experienced outside the walls of the church is far more accessible and tangible than what is offered inside. If religion can silence God inside the church, witchcraft can illuminate darkness outside the church. Witchcraft screams the church must grow brighter as the world grows darker. Witchcraft demands that God is only as powerful as his people. Afterall, witchcraft would assert that as many hypocrites are found at church as one would find on their average shopping trip. Witchcraft attempts to tie the moves of God to the actions of people and creates atmospheres where moves of God are perceived as 'weird' or even 'demonic,' as people have only seen these types of manifestations from occult practices.

The third lie most encountered from witchcraft demons happens within the church gathering. As thoughts creep into congregations about the necessity or even validity of the manifestations of God, fear rears its head within the heart of the church. Witchcraft opens the door for the spirit of fear to proclaim to the Church that it is better for God not to move than for people to be unsettled by his movements. This lie is the perfect union of religion and witchcraft. Fear within the Church leads to lack of exposure outside the church. If the churched is silenced, even the most subtle moves of witchcraft are amplified throughout the heavenlies. The world begins to focus more on what evil is happening in the world than on the good established by Jesus on the cross. We've all heard the greatest manifestation of this lie and may even be guilty of speaking it ourselves, 'If God is so good, then why does all of this evil exist in the world today? If God is love, then why is there so much hate? If God is who he says that he is, then why must sin exist?' Powerless God; tangible devils.

<u>Truth</u>

Witchcraft goes far beyond idolatry and spells. When we speak ill towards a person, we are cursing that person. Word curses are the most prominent form of witchcraft. When we consider how prevalent gossip is within our society, it's alarming to realize how rampant witchcraft really is among us.

Often times, we can say the right words to be appealing to our audience, yet be operating out of the wrong spirit.

Acts 16:16-18 - As we were going to the place of prayer, we were met by a slave girl who had a spirit of divination and brought her owners much gain by fortune-telling. She followed Paul and us, crying out, "These men are servants of the Most High God, who proclaim to you the way of salvation." And this she kept doing for many days. Paul, having become greatly annoyed, turned and said to the spirit, "I command you in the name of Jesus Christ to come out of her." And it came out that very hour.

In this historical account from Acts, the slave girl was speaking truthful words. She was making known that Paul was proclaiming the way of salvation from God. However, even though the words being spoken were pure on the surface level, they were laden with demonic poison. Paul casts the spirit of divination out of the girl setting her free, but causing much turmoil within the city. This leads to Paul being beaten and imprisoned.

Discerning of spirits is the only way to know by what spirit people are operating. Recall from chapter six that spirits click. If we are oblivious to the spirits working around us, we will be ineffective in impacting our spiritual environments.

1 Corinthians 2:11 - For who knows a person's thoughts except the spirit of that person, which is in him? So also no one comprehends the thoughts of God except the Spirit of God

When the Holy Spirit lives inside of us, however, he is capable of seeing what is occuring in the spirit realm in those who are around us.

Matthew 9:4 - But Jesus, knowing their thoughts, said, "Why do you think evil in your hearts?

Discernment, or the distinguishing of spirits, is a gift of the Holy Spirit which must be operational in the life of any believer who desires to be effectively engaged in spiritual warfare.

I will testify that our bodies often react to the presence of witchcraft as well. I have not been able to explain it yet, but when witchcraft has taken place against my life I often will feel unquenchably tired. I now know that if I find myself constantly exhausted or just cannot seem to stay awake when I should be able to, then I begin to pray for discerning the operation of witchcraft.

Commissioning Decree

A commission to aid in warfare against witchcraft in our lives:

In the name of Jesus Christ I bind up every vain imagination and thought.

I cast down every mental locution that would exalt itself above the name of Jesus.

I release the angels to come alongside this word and push back the influence of witchcraft over my life and region.

I bind every hindering spirit that would oppose these words.

I bind up witchcraft and say that false authority and demonic power has no hold over my life.

Jesus is the way, the truth, and the life and his Holy Spirit is the only spirit I accept in my life to provide my guidance and provision.

I am filled within my heart and sealed with the Holy Spirit by my salvation.

I receive the fullness of the Holy Spirit, so much of God in my life that I cannot contain it and it overflows into every aspect of my daily living.

By the overflow, the baptism of the Holy Spirit, I receive power from on high; I live with the fruits and giftings of the Holy Spirit.

I receive distinguishing of spirits by the one true Spirit to know by what motives people engage in my life.

I will not fall prey to lies and deception; my eyes are set to only see the truth.

The blood of Jesus covers my life and I will be free from all demonic oppression.

In the salvation gifted to me by Jesus Christ is the provision for the deliverance of my spirit from every demon of witchcraft.

I receive around my life discernment through the supernatural gifting of the Holy Spirit and other believers in which I trust.

God, I thank you for wisdom is found in sound council.

I pray favor over those who are my spiritual covering and who pour into my life.

I declare they will have godly insight and direction for me.

I receive breaker anointing from those who cover me.

God I believe the truth of your word.

I thank you that Peter was divinely inspired by Holy Spirit to author two letters and I know that the truths he revealed to them are still applicable to my life today.

I declare 2 Peter 1:2-4 over my life today:

2 Peter 1:2-4 - May grace and peace be multiplied to you in the knowledge of God and of Jesus our Lord. His divine power has granted to us all things that pertain to life and godliness, through the knowledge of him who called us to his own glory and excellence, by which he has granted to us his precious and very great promises, so that through them you may become partakers of the divine nature, having escaped from the corruption that is in the world because of sinful desire.

Testimony

Not every encounter with witchcraft is seen face-to-face. The most intense battle I've experienced with demons of witchcraft was seen in the spirit and dealt with in the spirit. Trust me, that is not for a lack of personal encounters with witchcraft either. Even while authoring this particular chapter, inside of the office next to mine there are individuals who are calling forth necromancers, casting spells, and summoning forth all sorts of demons.

The most intense battle against witchcraft began with an unction that what we were experiencing was not up to God's standard. Our life in the natural felt much more like striving than living from the promises of God. Our church was in a slump, our bi-vocational Worship Pastor had been without a primary income job for far too long, and many others were experiencing odd happenings. As my wife Natalie began having more in depth discussions with one of our members, it was revealed to her that the young woman's past had many ties to witchcraft. The young woman's mother even claimed to have once killed an individual through witchcraft. The Holy Spirit gifted Natalie with discernment and she knew that not only these demonic ties needed broken off of this young woman's life, but that this coven of witches had made direct spiritual attacks against our church as one of 'their own' was being set free.

We called for an impromptu prayer meeting and worship night. In the spirit, it got ugly that night. Warfare is not orderly. As we've all heard the cliche stands true, all is fair in love in war. When we are truly worshipping God in love or violently attacking the enemy, it can look ugly. Tears, cries, and praise filled our house that night; something broke in the spirit realm.

Nearly immediately after that night our Worship Pastor was offered a job that he was passionate about. Our church stepped into the next season of growth and breakthrough. That young woman's life has never been the same. There were several others who there that night also. One other young woman has since gone on to become extremely well known across the globe and her business is more successful than it ever was prior. Every single person who was in attendance that night experienced some sort of supernatural provision or breakthrough afterwards.

I never saw that coven of witches. No one in attendance that night did either. Witchcraft had been done by them against our church, yet none of us saw that personally. However, the word curses were broken off individuals and our local church that night. The spiritual effects of that night were seen by everyone. Our battle is not against flesh and blood so at times we may only deal with attacks in the spirit.

Prayer

As I suggested in the previous chapter, I will suggest again and forevermore: pray in tongues to get in position for what God is doing in this moment to break off witchcraft, demonic oppression, and all side effects. Unashamedly get violent in the spirit.

Matthew 11:12 - From the days of John the Baptist until now the kingdom of heaven has suffered violence, and the violent take it by force.

Warfare is not sophisticated, but it is strategic. Cast down the demons that would be so bold as to come against a child of God. With tongues of angels command the angels to war on our behalf and tell the demons to bow before the name of Jesus.

Father, I come to you in the name of Jesus. God I thank you that you are the ultimate power and authority.

Jesus I thank you that all power and authority was given to you by the Father during your time here on earth. I'm thankful that you greatly stewarded that authority; you became a role model for how to live our lives here on this earth. I thank you that you gifted your authority to men and you gifted us your Spirit to have the capability of handling so much authority. God I thank you that through those disciples, your authority and power has been passed down through the generations inside your Church to me. I believe that the same Spirit that raised Christ Jesus now lives in me according to your word as is found in Romans 8:11.

Holy Spirit, it is by your presence and power that I am capable of making such bold moves in the spirit. It is your Spirit within me that elevates me to a place to conduct warfare on such high levels. It is your authority that causes every knee to bow and every tongue to confess Jesus as Lord. No angel nor demon has more authority from you. In the best scheme of the devil, he was only capable of stealing one-third of your influence. Even by theft he could not gain an equal amount of authority to you God. With that authority I pray.

In the name of Jesus I cast off every demonic oppression that has come forth out of witchcraft. I rebuke every demonic oppression over my life that has come by demons and spirits of witchcraft. I break every word curse and spell that has been spoken against me. I command the devil to repay back all that he has stolen from my life with interest because what I own is blessed by the Lord. I rebuke every spirit of delay and call these things forth to occur in this kairos moment. The spirit realm is not delayed by chronological time and I deny every delay in the spirit realm right now in the name of Jesus.

Jesus! Jesus! Jesus! May your name be lifted high in the church and across the globe. Lay low every demon that would attempt to exalt itself against you Jesus. I pray these things in your name Jesus. Amen.

Chapter 10:
Warfare - Seducing spirits

Seducing spirits had more control over my life than any other demonic stronghold. I was exposed to pornography at a very early age. I was taught that I should seek to be with as many women as possible prior to marriage. I was even shoved into sexual situations by those who were called to protect my intimacy.

When I met Jesus, I was free from all sin and bondage, but my environment was not. I truly desired to follow Jesus with my entire being. However, I did not know how to break the strongholds of seducing spirits off of my life. While religion and witchcraft are the ringleaders when it comes to demonic spirits, seducing spirits have some of the greatest reach, especially in North America.

When I got saved, I attempted to confess my sins to my brothers for accountability that I may be forgiven and set free. Unfortunately, their immaturity caused them to share those intimate details of my life with other "friends" and even relationships I was attempting to establish. That did not cause me to stop seeking freedom though.

I went to the man who led me to Christ and confessed that I was struggling sexually. He got very frustrated with me and questioned my salvation. He scolded me and informed me that if I was really saved that a fruit of the Holy Spirit is self-control and I would no longer struggle with those things. He said he had been set free and I should have been by that point as well. I should have retorted that the same Spirit gives the manifestational gifts and I did not see those prevelanent in his life, but I humbly kept silent. I also stayed un-healed.

The spirits of religion empower seducing spirits to continue their hold on believers within the church. Religion wanted me to know that Jesus was real and the Savior, yet attempt to fool me into thinking that his sacrifice could not set me free in every area of my life. If I would believe that lie, then perhaps he could even deceive me into believing that Jesus' sacrifice could not save everyone.

Regardless of the sin, its significance, or its withstanding in our lives, Jesus' sacrifice on the cross was and still is sufficient. Every time we allow sin to have room in our lives and we believe we cannot overcome that sin, we diminish the sacrifice of Jesus. Every time we hold onto unforgiveness in our lives, especially towards ourselves, we worship Satan. When we believe that we are not worthy of our own forgiveness, we are telling Jesus that what he did was not good enough for our lives in that area. When we believe the lie that the work on the cross was not enough for us, we bow down in the spirit before Satan and confess that he is more powerful than Jesus' blood.

Description

When it comes to seducing spirits, one name stands out among all the others, Jezebel.

Revelation 2:20 - But I have this against you, that you tolerate that woman Jezebel, who calls herself a prophetess and is teaching and seducing my servants to practice sexual immorality and to eat food sacrificed to idols.

I believe the Church has subconsciously began to tolerate Jezebel because we seek her out. For instance, my Dad lives three hours away so I never expect him to show up to our local church on Sunday mornings. On the other hand, Natalie's grandmother is a member of our church so I expect her to be there weekly. People we expect to see show up far more often than those we do not. Furthermore, there are some individuals who I know will never walk through the doors of our church because I do not tolerate their behavior. By seeking out Jezebel, by expecting her to show up in the local church, we've created an atmosphere where she is welcome; we've tolerated her. While Jezebel is a serious threat as Jesus prophesied to the modern church, she is not the only seducing spirit.

The most ruthless seducing demon in Scripture next to Jezebel is Delilah. After having slept with multiple prostitutes, Samson opens the door for Delilah. More than once, Delilah bound Samson up and tormented him throughout the night. Sexual spirits, incubus and succubus, will attack us while we sleep.

Judges 16:16 - And when she pressed him hard with her words day after day, and urged him, his soul was vexed to death.

Delilah controlled Samson and forced him to sleep in her lap. Seducing spirits will weaken us physically in an attempt to move us spiritually to a place of vulnerability.

Seducing spirits are not just sexual seduction. Demons can seduce through temptation and coveting as well. If it moods us to move, it is seducing. Alluring, tempting, and enticing are all words that give the depiction of what seduction looks like in the natural. Pride is very seductive in nature.

Psalm 73:6 - Therefore pride is their necklace; violence covers them as a garment.

Those filled with pride and arrogance fall to this deception because they have been seduced with feelings that their lifestyle is captivating and most are unworthy of their presence. Consequently, Mammon makes money seductive. Money should simply be a tool for exchange, but it has often been corrupted by seduction: sexual immorality, drugs, and pride.

Lie

The greatest lie of seducing spirits is an attempt to get believers to believe that all sin is equal. While all sin has the same effect of removing us from the presence of God and death for unbelievers, not all sin cost Jesus the same on the cross.

1 Corinthians 6:18 - Flee from sexual immorality. Every other sin a person commits is outside the body, but the sexually immoral person sins against his own body.

Sexual sin harms the body in a way unlike any other sin. Even in the Old Covenant, different sins cost the individual different portions of their inheritance. We see this in part in Leviticus chapter four where the unintentional sins of the congregation cost a bull, the unintentional sins of the leader cost an unblemished male goat, and the unintentional sins of the common person cost a female goat without blemish.

Sexual sin is a sin against self (1 Corinthians 6:18). A female's reproductive system was engineered by God to mold to her spouse; something it is unable to do successfully if the woman has multiple partners. Sexual sin also becomes addictive and creates soul ties.

1 Corinthians 6:16 - Or do you not know that he who is joined to a prostitute becomes one body with her? For, as it is written, "The two will become one flesh."

Every time we lay sexually with an individual, our flesh becomes one. This also creates what is commonly referred to as a soul tie. When our flesh becomes one, our souls become intermingled. The Bible recognizes that a man and a woman in a marital covenant are no longer two distinct individuals but one. This is not merely a joining of the flesh, but a uniting of the souls. The mind, will, and emotions of these individuals are now intertwined as well. This happens through pornography as well.

When we examine sexual immorality, we quickly see that the individual harms their own self because they are spiritually torn to pieces. Every individual we unite with sexually we give them part of our soul. When we are sexually active with multiple partners (even if it is only one at a time), our soul is divided among all these individuals. To make matters worse, if soul ties are not disposed of, not only do we unite our soul with the individual we lay with but also every individual who their soul has tied to previously. Sexual sin is the most dangerous sin we can commit as it destroys the mind.

If soul ties have been discovered by reading this book, there is still hope for the believer. Jesus restores all. His covenant and blood are stronger than any demonic covenant we have formed. Repent of false beliefs and ask for all of our soul to be restored to us fully and give others soul back to them.

Truth

Beauty is not bad. Esther was chosen by God to fulfill a very divine role due to her beauty.

Esther 2:7 - He was bringing up Hadassah, that is Esther, the daughter of his uncle, for she had neither father nor mother. The young woman had a beautiful figure and was lovely to look at, and when her father and her mother died, Mordecai took her as his own daughter.

Sexual immorality is not caused by attraction; it is caused by lust. A thought which arise in the mind does not equate to sin; dwelling on that thought does. As males and females we were both created in the image of God, we are attractive. Males and females were designed by God for intimacy. We are attractive to each other. It is a covenant to enter into marriage with one of the opposite sex before God to enjoy that intimacy in a manner that is not just pleasing to God, but worship to him. God devoted one entire book of the Bible for us to understand healthy sexual etiquette (Song of Solomon) and it is a regularly discussed subject throughout Scripture.

Secondly, seduction is not necessary for intimacy.

Genesis 2:25 - And the man and his wife were both naked and were not ashamed.

God created male and female, Adam and Eve, to be completely and totally vulnerable to one another. There was no shame in their nakedness until sin entered the world. Prior to their sin, they were intimate with one another and their differences were always exposed. Seduction hides our intimacies and allures the others to want to see our intimacies. However, in a healthy marital covenant, husband and wife are capable of being naked and vulnerable with one another without shame.

Cosmetics were introduced to the world as a beauty enhancement that allured men into sexual temptation as an act of demonic worship. Let me stop there and say makeup is not inherently evil. My wife is a professional makeup artist. However, I must be attracted to her not a facade or masquerade of who she can be in the moment. The greatest hindrance to marriages is the incapability of spouses to be unashamed before one another with all their differences exposed.

To reiterate this point, seduction is security for false intimacy. When one is made to be more attractive through enhancements (cosmetics, clothing, surgery, etc.), that individual is perverting their natural beauty. When sex is initiated solely because of this enhanced beauty, the sex is driven by seduction not intimacy. Seduction will get us physically closer than any other act, while at the same time creating a barrier which prohibits intimacy and dissasimilates our soul.

Commissioning Decree

A commission to aid in warfare against seducing demons in our lives:

In the name of Jesus Christ I bind up every vain imagination and thought.

I cast down every mental locution that would exalt itself above the name of Jesus.

I release the angels to come alongside this word and push back the influence of seduction over my life and region.

I bind every hindering spirit that would oppose these words.

I bind up false intimacy and say that no demon is allowed to allure me into temptation.

My heart is set upon doing the Lord's will
and nothing can seduce me into compromising that.

I will not covet the goods of my neighbor nor
will I lust after his love.

I receive distinguishing of spirits by the one
true Spirit to know by what motives people engage
in my life.

I will not fall prey to lies and deception; my
eyes are set to only see the truth.

My eyes were created to long upon one
God and one person who I hold to in a covenant
before my God.

The blood of Jesus covers my life and I will
be free from all demonic oppression.

In the salvation gifted to me by Jesus Christ
is the provision for the deliverance of my spirit from
every demon of seduction.

I cast off the influence of Jezebel, Delilah,
pride, Mammon, and all other seducing spirits off of
my life.

I receive around my life discernment
through the supernatural gifting of the Holy Spirit
and other believers in which I trust.

God, I thank you for wisdom is found in
sound council.

I pray favor over those who are my spiritual
covering and who pour into my life.

I declare they will have godly insight and
direction for me.

I receive breaker anointing from those who
cover me.

God I believe the truth of your word.

I thank you Father for Jesus' apostolic
prayer to you and I know that the truths he revealed
to them are still applicable to my life today.

I declare Matthew 6:13 over my life today:

Matthew 6:13 - And lead us not into temptation, but deliver us from evil. You do not lead us into temptation Lord, but you do deliver us from all evil!

Testimony

Seducing spirits kept a stronghold in my life for far too long. The only thing that could truly break their power was love. The love of God contained in even just one drop of the blood of Jesus is powerful enough to rid every demon and sin from someone's life. However, most of us need to experience this love flowing through an individual in order to truly be set free.

Jesus responded to his disciples privately in Mark chapter nine that some demons can only be cast out by prayer. I would add that some wounds can only be healed by the individual who has dominion over that area in our lives. Let me explain. We were created to be in a sexual covenant with one individual on this planet. I have seen individuals who never experienced true forgiveness and healing from sexual sin until their spouse was able to walk them through those areas, my life being one of those. Our spouse is the ultimate spiritual authority over our sex life on this planet next to God. The forgiveness of a spouse from sexual sin is the most resounding noise a seducing spirit will ever hear.

I was only able to walk away from all sexual sin in my life once I experienced true love and forgiveness from Natalie. When I was naked and not ashamed before her, when I was vulnerable and honest with my weaknesses, and she still chose to love me, I saw what true love was in the life of an individual. Agape (Godly) love was no longer a theory, but was looking at me in the face. As we confessed these sins to our pastors and I experienced it yet again, our marriage covenant become solidified in purity and honor.

1 Peter 4:8 - Above all, keep loving one another earnestly, since love covers a multitude of sins.

Love was not meant to sweep sin under the rug, but true love will always overcome sin and destroy strongholds. Generosity breaks the yoke every time.

1 Corinthians 13:1 - If I speak in the tongues of men and of angels, but have not love, I am a noisy gong or a clanging cymbal.

As Paul wrote the first letter to the church at Corinth, he was very aware that their culture before Jesus was polytheistic. The temples surrounding them were for multiple gods and the services were both seductive and a mockery of true worship. Paul interestingly chose the gong and cymbal for a reason. These instruments were used in the temples for worship of demons. If our spiritual gifts are not saturated in love, then we have been seduced by demonic spirits and are prostituting the gifts of the Holy Spirit.

Prayer

As I suggested previously, pray in tongues to get in position for what God is doing in this moment to break off the works of seducing spirits in and around our lives. Be prepared to be naked and unashamed before God and spouse if that is the season.

Father, I come to you in the name of Jesus. God I thank you that when you created mankind, you created Adam and Eve naked to walk in your presence without shame. Father, I pray that you restore that same vulnerability in my relationship with you through Jesus name.

Jesus, I thank you that no amount of clothing nor temptation seduced you into hiding yourself from the Father. I'm thankful that you Jesus walked in perfect unison with Father and Spirit throughout your duration here on earth. I believe that you modeled the perfect life here on earth and then sent your Spirit to guide me to do the same.

Holy Spirit, thank you for overflowing into every area of my life. Protect my eyes as they are the gateway to my soul. Holy Spirit convict me; do not allow me to fulfill the lusts of my flesh. Keep my emotions, will, and mind in submission to your guidance. I renounce all soul ties I have formed through sexual sin and ask that you deliver my spirit from the temptation of the devil.

In the name of Jesus, I break off all affliction and alure caused by seducing spirits over my life. I break all soul ties and recommit the covenant relationship that I have with Christ Jesus. The covenant I have with God is stronger than any man-made covenant or covenant I have formed with demonic spirits. My soul is free and totally committed to pursuing the love of my life which is Jesus. I am his bride and he is my bridegroom. My eyes are set upon my love and I will not be tempted to lust after the pleasures of this world. My flesh was created for procreation, to fill the earth and subdue it, yet my flesh is empowered by the Spirit of God to birth the fruit of self control. I produce this fruit by abiding in Jesus; there is no striving in my life.

I recommit my spirit to you Jesus. I renounce any open doors that seduction has given to other demons. I specifically renounce all generational curses and command they are to be broken at the time I was born again. I close the door to seducing spirits, witchcraft, and religion in my life. I shut every demonic entryway in the name of Jesus. Holy Spirit I open the door for you to fill every part of my being. Fill even the crevices which were created by demonic presence in my life.

I welcome the angels of the Lord to come minister to me just as they ministered to you Jesus. Make me more sensitive to their presence. Create a yearning in me to long to see your manifestations outnumber those of demons around my life.

Finally, may the Spirit of God living in me become irresistible to those who are called to you Jesus. May I become a beacon of your hope and a disciple who makes disciples who make disciples. For every temptation and flaming dart hurled my way by demons may it cost the devil at minimum one soul paid immediately from an eternity in hell. Jesus, I pray all of this in your name. Amen.

Appendices

Appendix A:
Angels

Below is a list of angels with Scriptural reference as I have found them in the Bible. I by no means believe this list to be all-encompassing, but may it grant you favor and wisdom in your pursuit of the supernatural. Each spirit listed in alphabetical order and is only provided with at least one reference.

Angel of His Presence	*Isaiah 63:9*
Angel of the Lord	*Isaiah 37:36*
Archangel	*1 Thessalonians 4:16*
Burning/Purging	*Isaiah 4:4*
Confusion	*Isaiah 19:14*
Counsel and Might	*Isaiah 11:2*
Deep Sleep	*Isaiah 29:10*
Gabriel	*Daniel 8:16, 9:21; Luke 1:19, 26*
Gentle	*1 Peter 3:4*
"Guardian"	*Matthew 18:10*
Heavenly Host	*Luke 2:13*
Judgement	*Isaiah 4:4*
Justice	*Isaiah 28:4*
Knowledge and Fear of the Lord	*Isaiah 11:2*

Michael	*Jude 1:9; Revelation 12:7*
Quiet	*1 Peter 3:4*
Revelation	*Ephesians 1:17*
Seraphim	*Isaiah 6:2*
Skill	*Exodus 28:3*
Slumber/Stuper	*Romans 11:8*
Twelve Legions	*Matthew 26:53*
Wisdom	*Ephesians 1:17*
Wisdom and Understanding	*Isaiah 11:2*

Appendix B:
Demons

Below is a list of fallen angels, or demons, with Scriptural reference as I have found them in the Bible. I by no means believe this list to be all-encompassing, but may it grant you favor and wisdom in your pursuit of the supernatural. Each spirit listed in alphabetical order and is only provided with at least one reference.

This list was comprised by those obviously listed in Scripture. For instance, I believe Cain was lead by a critical spirit in Genesis 4:1-16 which influenced him to murder his brother. This spirit causes those under its influence to be critical of self, critical of overs, and to falsely believe others are overly critical as well. It is the opposite of the Holy Spirit which is a covenant Spirit. However, this generational spirit is not listed below.

Absalom   2 Samuel 14
Antichrist   1 John 4:3
Arpad   Isaiah 36:19
Artemis (of Ephesus)   Acts 19:28

Spiritual Forces of Evil	*Ephesians 6:11-12*
Unclean	*Luke 4:33*
Uncleanness	*Zechariah 13:2*
Viper	*Matthew 23:33*
Whoredom/Harlotry	*Hosea 4:12*
Women like Delilah	*Judges 12-16*
World	*1 Corinthians 2:12*

Made in the USA
Lexington, KY
27 November 2019